A PRACTICAL SYSTEM OF

BOOK-KEEPING

BY SINGLE AND DOUBLE ENTRY.

Deliver all things in number and weight, and put all in writing that thou givest out or receivest in.—ECCLESIASTICUS xlii. 7.

BY IRA MAYHEW, A. M.,

AUTHOR OF A TREATISE ON POPULAR EDUCATION.

NEW-YORK:

PUBLISHED BY DANIEL BURGESS & CO.,

(LATE CADY & BURGESS.)

60 JOHN-STREET.

SOLD BY BOOKSELLERS THROUGHOUT THE UNITED STATES.

1853.

ACCOUNT BOOKS.

A SET of Account Books has been prepared to accompany this volume, of sufficient size for entering all the Examples for Practice it contains, consisting of

I. A LEDGER FOR THE FIRST FORM OF ACCOUNTS. One Book, price eight cents.

II. A LEDGER FOR THE SECOND FORM OF ACCOUNTS. One Book, price eight cents.

III. A DAY-BOOK AND LEDGER FOR THE THIRD FORM OF ACCOUNTS. Two Books, price sixteen cents.

IV. A JOURNAL AND LEDGER FOR DOUBLE ENTRY. Two Books, price sixteen cents.

These Account Books have been prepared expressly to accompany this volume, are of convenient size and properly ruled, and cost but little more than the same amount of common paper.

Entered according to Act of Congress,
in the year one thousand eight hundred and fifty-one, by
IRA MAYHEW,
In the Clerk's Office of the District Court of the United States for the District of Michigan.

MAYHEW ON POPULAR EDUCATION:

A NEW NATIONAL WORK

FOR THE USE OF PARENTS AND TEACHERS,

AND FOR

YOUNG PERSONS OF BOTH SEXES.

See notices of this work on Popular Education at the 143d page of the Book-keeping; also notices of the Book-keeping at the 144th page.

STEREOTYPED BY
RICHARD C. VALENTINE,
17 Dutch-st., cor. of Fulton.

C. A. ALVORD, Printer,
29 Gold-street.

PREFACE.

AGESILAUS, king of Sparta, being asked what things he thought most proper for boys to learn, very appropriately replied, Those things which they should *practice* when they become men. Ever since it was said to Adam, In the sweat of thy face shalt thou eat bread, there has been a necessity laid upon man not only to *labor*, but to *exchange* with others the products of his industry, in order to secure a comfortable support. " Deliver all things in number and weight, and put in writing that thou givest out or receivest in," is a precept of universal application, and there is a special necessity for its observance in all business transactions between debtor and creditor. But excepting merchants, mechanics, and professional men, very few, comparatively, keep any accounts. The principal reason for this is found in the fact, that when young they were not taught how to do so, and the necessity of its being done. Considerations are presented in the Introduction to this work, to show some of the many advantages that would result to individuals and to the community from making Book-keeping a common study in all our schools. But our many excellent treatises on the subject seem very generally to have been prepared for the express use of persons who intend to engage in extensive business operations. The design of the present, on the contrary, is to furnish a practical system of popular Book-keeping, whose aim is to meet the wants of the great majority of the American people.

I. M.

MONROE, Mich., Sept., 1851.

iii

CONTENTS.

INTRODUCTION.

Book-keeping, which is the art of keeping accounts in such a manner that a person may at any time know the true state of his business, is necessary for every person engaged in the ordinary pursuits of life—for the day-laborer, the farmer, and the mechanic, as well as for professional men and persons engaged in mercantile pursuits.

If persons generally would keep correct accounts, they would be less likely to run into debt beyond their ability to pay; temptations to dishonesty would be diminished; there would be far less litigation among neighbors and those who have occasion to transact business with one another; habits of industry, frugality, and integrity would become more general; and in these and various other ways the social and moral virtues would be cultivated, and individuals generally, composing the community, would become more fraternal and humane.

As an illustration of the *moral* benefits that would result from keeping an exact account of one's personal expenses, it is sufficient to refer to the fact that individuals sometimes excuse themselves from keeping such an account, by saying it is not always pleasant to see, afterward, for what they have foolishly paid their money. This is doubtless true of more persons than have the frankness to make the confession. Others are unwilling to let their books show how, or for what, money or property has come into their possession. It can hardly be set down as uncharitable to infer that such love darkness rather than light, because their deeds are evil, and fear the light of correct entries, lest their deeds should be reproved. It must be apparent to every one, that all such persons need the *restraints* imposed by keeping an exact account of receipts and disbursements. Book-keeping, then, should be studied in every common school in the country, (as well as in all our higher seminaries of learning,) by young persons of both sexes.

Heretofore Book-keeping has rarely been studied except by young men who have expected to engage in mercantile pursuits. But if it was understood and practiced by women as well as by men, it would in many cases (and very properly, too,) render them more frugal in their personal and domestic expenses; prevent vast accumulations of indebtedness; diminish greatly the number of bankruptcies in the country; and secure to families generally the benefits resulting from living within their means. It would, moreover, exert a healthful influence upon the mind, and afford rational employment for many upon whom time hangs heavily, or is worse than thrown away in idleness and thoughtless dissipation.

While upon the husband, father, or brother, rests the duty of providing for the necessities, comforts, and conveniences of the family—upon the wife, daughter, or sister, devolves the scarcely less responsible office of judiciously expending the means furnished, in so far at least as the well-being of the household requires. This is by common consent regarded as coming within her appropriate sphere. It is then properly a part of the housewife's business to keep an account of all moneys expended by her for the benefit of the family, or on its behalf. When she does this, she becomes more fully a *help meet* for man, than it is possible for her otherwise to be. Domestic broils and family feuds not unfrequently result, either from real or supposed scanty provision on the part of the husband, or from alleged extravagance on the part of the wife. In case an account of the family expenses is kept as here suggested, the wife can at any time render an account for all moneys that have passed through her hands. Where the husband keeps a proper account of his business, it is hence easy to see when it may become necessary to curtail expenses in order to live within their means. It is evident, moreover, that under such circumstances two whose destinies are united for life, can more rationally confer together in relation to the well-being of the household, than where no such accounts are kept. I may here also venture one additional suggestion intimately connected with the preceding.

The wife or daughter might in many instances very properly keep the books of the husband or father, whose time is absorbed in the pursuits of a laborious profession, and thus not only save the expense of a clerk, but do the business more satisfactorily, and have the pleasure of contributing to the comfort and happiness of the family, as well as to its pecuniary interests. It is generally claimed (and with a fitness that I will not question) that there is quite too much *sewing* practiced, especially in all the higher walks of civic life. *Woman*, in this department of industry, is peculiarly the sufferer. Day after day, and night after night, she not unfrequently toils on, with but a scanty means of subsistence, her vitality wasting away, as, stitch after stitch, she overtasks her already exhausted energies, in the services of a mercenary employer, whose cupidity has beggared her children.

Book-keeping, at present practiced to a limited extent by females employed as milliners, clerks, or merchants, offers to the sex an asylum from these wrongs. Whatever may be said in relation to costume, and the fitness of the intermingling of the sexes on the political arena, none can for a moment question the propriety of woman's entering the counting-room and engaging in its quiet duties, for the discharge of which she is as well fitted by nature as the sterner sex. Females are now quite too dependent upon the kindly attentions of their male friends, if such they chance to have. Frequently, too frequently, alas! there is exhibited the painful spectacle of the *widow*, bereft of him to whom she has been accustomed to look for support and the maintenance of her little ones, without any knowledge of the ordinary forms of business, and hence not only without the means of procuring a competency for herself and children, but unable advantageously to assume the charge of any property she may chance to possess. Under such circumstances, few females, comparatively, are prepared properly to look to their own business. Losses, embarrassments, poverty, and not unfrequently the painful sense of dependence upon the cold charities of an unfeeling world, too often hasten those thus situated, who but yesterday were confiding and full of hope, *on* to a premature death, leaving the world sorrowful and broken-hearted, chiefly because of a defective education. How important it is, then, that the study under consideration should receive the attention of females as well as of males. Especially should Book-keeping be regarded as an indispensable study in every young ladies' seminary.

The one great object which parents seek to attain in directing their children to enter upon the study of arithmetic in our schools, and which youth have in view in entering upon it, is, that they may become the better qualified for the discharge of the ordinary duties of life and for the transaction of such business as they may have occasion to engage in. But if a portion of the time ordinarily given to this study was judiciously bestowed upon a practical system of General Book-keeping, this important object would be much more speedily reached, and with vastly more pleasure to the learner.

I would not underrate the importance of arithmetic as a study in our primary institutions of learning. It has long and very properly been pursued, in all well regulated schools, by both boys and girls, whose education I insist should be regarded as exceedingly defective without a familiar acquaintance with its principles and their application to the ordinary transactions of life. But it is apparent that a practical familiarity with the principles of General Book-keeping is of much greater importance than the most perfect comprehension of the mysteries of square and cube root, of arithmetical and geometrical progression, of permutations and combinations, of the summation of an infinite series, etc., etc., to say nothing of the exploded rules of single and double position, and many others that might be enumerated.

English grammar, which is defined as the art of speaking and writing the English language with propriety and accuracy, is now very generally studied in our common schools. But in order to turn it to the greatest account, its principles should be practically applied, *in the school-room*, to accounts, and the ordinary business transactions of life.

Much attention is now very properly paid to penmanship in our schools. But it should be borne in mind that the great mass of the people employ this art chiefly for the purpose of recording business transactions and in business correspondence. How important, then, that correct forms and habits in these respects be early acquired! Pupils, it ought generally to be known, make the most rapid improvement in penmanship when engaged in writing something in which they are interested, and which they feel that they can afterward turn to practical account. It cannot fail to be apparent, then, that independently of the benefits already enumerated, pupils will make greater improvement in this useful art by devoting a portion of their time to practical accounts than by writing after set copies.

The author of this treatise, in the execution of a plan laid many years ago, and practically tested in the school-room, has sought to supply what many practical teachers with whom he has compared views upon the subject in various portions of the country, have hitherto considered a *desideratum*. The study of this work may be advantageously commenced as soon as the pupil is familiar with the fundamental rules of arithmetic ; and it may be successfully prosecuted in connection with any of the branches of an English education. The following are some of its distinguishing characteristics :

1. Before introducing the pupil to accounts in which debit and credit entries occur, which is usually the first thing done in

treatises on Book-keeping, a business transaction is defined, and the mode of entering the same in the books of both debtor and creditor illustrated. Several transactions are then stated, in various phraseology, and the entries to be made in the books of both parties further exemplified. These entries—which are in all cases made in *script* that closely resembles *writing*—afford good *models* for the learner. Then, in the first example of accounts that is presented, the transactions entered are on the same folio stated in common language, which enables the learner fully to comprehend the whole matter.

2. After giving a few specimens of the mode of keeping accounts by the first and simplest form, (four forms are presented in this treatise,) together with the necessary instructions to the learner, a series of *business transactions*, drawn from the ordinary pursuits of life, are introduced, in the form of *problems to be solved*. In their solution it becomes necessary, from inspecting the transactions, merely, to compute the value of whatever has been bought or sold, the price and the quantity being given ; to make the requisite debit and credit entries, after first determining to which side of the account each transaction belongs ; and then to balance the several accounts, which are to be written out like the patterns already set, and entered in a blank-book prepared for that purpose. Numerous examples for practice are likewise introduced, in each of the remaining forms of account, with accompanying blank-books appropriately ruled, in which they are to be entered when solved.

3. In every form of accounts introduced, the necessary instructions having been given to the learner, accompanied by a series of problems to be solved by the student, the requisite suggestions are given to enable classes to keep sets of books based upon transactions of their own entry. In this way they approach more nearly the actual business transactions of life than by any other method with which I am acquainted. Indeed, throughout the entire treatise, the examples are as practi-

cal as they possibly can be, where the learner is not actually the salesman.

4. The instructions in relation to the mode of keeping accounts, which will be found sufficiently full for all ordinary purposes, are generally given on the same page or folio with the illustrative examples, with carefully prepared questions for the examination of classes.

5. For the convenience of teachers in examining the work of their classes, as well as for the encouragement of the private learner, a Key has been prepared to accompany this work, in which all the examples for practice are correctly entered in the various books used, and the accounts balanced and closed, so that no teacher, however inexperienced in keeping accounts, need shrink from undertaking to instruct classes in the use of this book.

These characteristics are believed to be peculiar to this work. They make the whole subject perfectly intelligible to the intermediate classes in our common schools, as well as to those more advanced, and invest it with so much of interest as to render it highly attractive. In its use, it is confidently believed scholars will more rapidly acquire that facility in making business computations which is most desirable, than by devoting the same time exclusively to the study of arithmetic, as has hitherto been generally practiced; that they will make greater proficiency in penmanship than though an equal amount of time were devoted to writing after set copies; and that they will at the same time more readily acquire a thorough and practical knowledge of Book-keeping than from the study of any work that has heretofore been given to the public. So, view it in what light we may, the advantages arising from the study of Book-keeping, with the improved methods here presented, are too great and too numerous to allow much time to elapse before its general introduction into all our common, intermediate, and high schools.

TO THE PUPIL.

From an attentive perusal of the preceding Introduction you will see some of the many benefits resulting to persons engaged in the various departments of productive industry, from the study and practice of Book-keeping. Others will present themselves to your mind in your progress through the book. As in other departments of study, so in this, while you can gain nothing desirable by leaving a subject imperfectly understood, you will really lose much. You should hence let it be a settled rule with you never to proceed onward while any thing remains unconquered behind. In order then to facilitate your progress in this important study, and to render it of the greatest practical utility, you will do well constantly to bear in mind the following suggestions, until you shall have formed correct *habits* in relation to the several particulars named.

1. Make every arithmetical calculation yourself, as you proceed. Rely not upon any result stated in the book, until you have first made the computation on which it depends; otherwise, although the *author* may have derived some discipline from its preparation, *you* certainly will gain little from its perusal. What is worth doing at all, is worth doing well.

2. In solving the Examples for Practice, exercise your *common sense* in determining how each transaction is to be entered; whether all on one side of the account, and if so, on which; or a part on one side of the account and a part on the other.

3. Spell every word correctly, and write neatly and legibly.

4. Study brevity and perspicuity in recording business transactions, and in business correspondence.

GENERAL BOOK-KEEPING.

BOOK-KEEPING is the art of keeping accounts in such a manner that a person may at any time know the true state of his business, or of his debts and credits, by an inspection of his books. The term General Book-keeping signifies that kind of book-keeping which is suitable for persons generally, such as farmers, mechanics, professional men, retailers, and, indeed, all persons except merchants engaged in a wholesale business.

If persons could universally receive an equivalent for their wares when sold, and were enabled to pay at the time for whatever they have occasion to purchase, it would still be desirable to keep a record of their business transactions. This necessity becomes imperative whenever products and goods are bought and sold without making payment at the time.

DEBTOR AND CREDITOR.

Whenever one person receives any thing from another, which he does not pay for at the time, he is said to *go in debt* for it, and is called a Debtor. A person who sells property without receiving his pay at the time, is said to *give credit* for it, and is called a Creditor. In other words, the *receiver* is always the Debtor, and the *giver* is always the Creditor. In keeping accounts it is customary, and more convenient, to abridge and write Dr. for Debtor, and Cr. for Creditor.

What is Book-keeping? What is meant by General Book-keeping? Is it always desirable to keep a record of business transactions? When does this necessity become imperative? When does a person become a Debtor? When a Creditor? When property exchanges hands without payment being made at the time, what general rule is stated in relation to the *receiver* and *giver* of it? What abbreviations are used for Debtor and Creditor?

The act of buying or selling is called a Transaction. In every transaction there must be both a *buyer* and a *seller*. Where the property which exchanges hands is not paid for at the time of the transfer, the buyer becomes a Debtor, and the seller a Creditor. The following will serve as an illustration of the correct use of the terms already employed:

TRANSACTION.—James Armitage buys of Isaac Merrill one pair of Kip boots, for which he is to pay him four dollars.

In this transaction James Armitage is the Debtor, because he is the *receiver;* and Isaac Merrill is the Creditor, because he is the *giver.*

The parties make the following entries in their respective books, under the date of the transaction:

Isaac Merrill writes in his book,

James Armitage,   *Dr.*

To one pair of Kip boots,   *$4.00*

James Armitage writes in his book,

Isaac Merrill,   *Cr.*

By one pair of Kip boots,   *$4.00*

By examining these entries the pupil will see that the creditor writes the debtor's name in his book, and that the debtor writes the creditor's name in his book. This should be remembered, for it constitutes an invariable rule.

The word *To,* with which the creditor commences the entry in his book, indicates the *passage* of whatever has been sold, from him *to* the debtor; and the word *By,* with which the

What is a Transaction? What must there be in every Transaction? Which becomes the Debtor, and which the Creditor? State a Transaction. In this Transaction who is the Debtor, and why? Who the Creditor, and why? In the Transaction stated, what entries should the parties make in their respective books? Whose name does the creditor write in his book? Whose name does the debtor write in his book? Why ought this to be remembered? What does the word *To*, with which the creditor commences the entry in his book, indicate? What the word *By*, with which the debtor commences the entry in his book?

14

debtor commences the entry in his book, the *reception by him* of that which the creditor has charged to him.

The following examples will further illustrate the mode of entering transactions in the books of both debtor and creditor, with which the pupil should become familiar before progressing further. For this purpose separate sheets of paper may be used. Let the pupil write the transactions on one page, numbering them, and make the proper entries on another page, with their corresponding numbers and correct dates, as in the annexed examples. The *transactions* may be copied from the book. The *entries* should be made like those in the examples given: but they should be made from *an examination of the transaction*, not copied from the book. The pupil might also write out additional transactions, and having studied them carefully, be prepared in recitation to give the entries either on the blackboard, in writing, or orally, all of which methods might in turn be practiced.

The *price* and the *quantity* being given, the learner should, from the first, invariably compute the *amount* of all articles bought or sold, whether the calculations are made in the book or not. It would be to his advantage to do this in studying any treatise on Book-keeping. But in the study of this work it is *absolutely necessary ;* for the pupil will soon be called upon to record transactions where such computations are unavoidable.

What computations should the learner invariably make ? Are such computations *avoidable* in the study of this treatise ?

State the first transaction, and give the entries to be made in the books of both parties. State the second transaction and the entries. The third, etc. Let the pupil state additional transactions, and give the entries orally, or on the blackboard.

SEVERAL TRANSACTIONS:

TRANSACTION 1. JANUARY 1.

James Armitage buys of Isaac Merrill one pair of Kip boots, for which he is to pay him four dollars.

James Armitage is the debtor, because he is the receiver. Isaac Merrill is the creditor, because he is the giver.

TRANSACTION 2. JANUARY 2.

Hallock & Raymond sell to John S. Barry one suit of clothes, for which he is to pay them fifty-two dollars.

John S. Barry is the debtor, because he is the receiver. Hallock & Raymond are the creditors, because they are the givers.

TRANSACTION 3. JANUARY 3.

Wm. H. Boyd sells to C. G. Johnson 40 lbs. of nails, for six cents a pound.

C. G. Johnson is the debtor, because he is the receiver. Wm. H. Boyd is the creditor, because he is the giver.

TRANSACTION 4. JANUARY 4.

Alex. McFarren buys of Harper & Brothers 4 doz. copies of Mayhew on Popular Education, at $9.00 a doz.

Alex. McFarren is the debtor, because he is the receiver. Harper and Brothers are the creditors, because they are the givers.

16

MODE OF ENTERING THEM.

Jan.	1	Isaac Merrill writes in his book, *James Armitage,* *Dr.* *To one pair of Kip boots,*		4	00
Jan.	1	James Armitage writes in his book, *Isaac Merrill,* *Cr.* *By one pair of Kip boots,*		4	00
Jan.	2	Hallock & Raymond write in their book, *John S. Barry,* *Dr.* *To one suit of clothes,*		52	00
Jan.	2	John S. Barry writes in his book, *Hallock & Raymond,* *Cr.* *By one suit of clothes,*		52	00
Jan.	3	Wm. H. Boyd writes in his book, *C. G. Johnson,* *Dr.* *To 40 lbs. of nails,*	.06	2	40
Jan.	3	C. G. Johnson writes in his book, *Wm. H. Boyd,* *Cr.* *By 40 lbs. of nails,*	.06	2	40
Jan.	4	Harper & Brothers write in their book, *Alex. McFarren,* *Dr.* *To 4 doz. Mayhew on Pop. Ed.*	9.00	36	00
Jan.	4	Alex. McFarren writes in his book, *Harper & Brothers,* *Cr.* *By 4 doz. Mayhew on Pop. Ed.*	9.00	3)	00

17

ACCOUNT BOOKS.

The number of books necessary, and the particular mode of keeping one's accounts, must depend upon the nature and extent of his business. Forms are sometimes given for Farmers; others, for Mechanics; and others still, for Merchants. But so great is the difference in the extent and variety of business carried on by these and other classes of persons, that some farmers find it desirable to keep a greater number of books than are requisite for mechanics; and other farmers, and mechanics, not unfrequently do a more varied and extensive business than is sometimes carried on by the merchant. In a treatise on General Book-keeping, then, it seems befitting to commence with the simplest form of accounts, which will be found convenient for persons engaged in a limited business of almost any kind, and afterward introduce others, and leave persons to select the form they shall deem best adapted to their particular business, taking into the account both its nature and extent.

Three forms for keeping accounts are presented in this treatise, in Single Entry, and one in Double Entry.

FIRST FORM OF ACCOUNTS.

The LEDGER, which is indispensable, even where the Day-book and Journal are used as preliminary books, is the most important book in general book-keeping, and the only one necessary in the first form of accounts. Its object is to show how the owner stands toward the various persons with whom he has credit transactions. Two pages opposite each other are appropriated for each individual account. The name of the

---

Upon what must the number of books used and the mode of keeping one's accounts depend? Why cannot particular forms be prescribed for Farmers, Mechanics, and Merchants? How many forms for keeping accounts are given in this treatise? What book only is necessary in the first form? Can the Ledger be dispensed with when the Day-book and Journal are used as preliminary books? What is the object of the Ledger?

person, and his residence, (if this is necessary to identify him,) should be written in a bold hand at the top of the page, or at the head of the account, for a title, as in the annexed examples. The left-hand page is devoted to the Dr. entries, and the right-hand page to the Cr. entries. Each page is divided by perpendicular lines into five spaces, in the first of which the year and month are entered; in the second, the day of the month; in the third, the items bought or sold; and in the fourth and fifth, their value in dollars and cents.

When a person has occasion to use several Ledgers, as all do who engage extensively in business, it is customary to designate them by the letters of the alphabet, thus: Ledger A; Ledger B; etc.

THE INDEX.

The Index is a small book in which the names of all persons having accounts in the Ledger, and the titles of accounts other than personal, are arranged in alphabetical order, under their initial letters, with reference to the folios or pages in which they stand. In the case of small Ledgers, the Index may be conveniently written in a few of the first pages of the Ledger: but where large Ledgers are used, it will be found more convenient to employ a separate Index.

When should the *residence* of a person be given in the title of his account, in connection with his name? When two pages are appropriated to an account, which is devoted to the Dr. entries? Which to the Cr. entries? Into how many spaces should each page be divided, and what should be entered in the several spaces? When a person has several Ledgers, how are they usually designated? What is the Index? When may it be kept in the Ledger?

A		H
Adams, Samuel	2	

B		I
Brown, James	1	
Bruce, John	3	

C		J
Cash Account	7	
Corn-field, 8 Acres	6	

D		K

E		L

F		M
		Martin, John	8

G		N

INDEX TO LEDGER A.

O		U	
P		V *Van Allen, Henry*	*9.8*
Q		W *Wheat Account* *Wheat-field, 18 Acres*	5 4
R		X	
S		Y	
T		Z	

When an account is transferred from one folio to another, as in the case of Henry Van Allen, both folios should be noted in the Index. This account, originally kept on the 8th folio, has been carried to the 9th.

When an account is transferred to a new folio, what should be noted in the Index?

James Brown $\mathcal{D}r.$

1850						
Jan.	5	To 4 Cords Hickory	1.75		7	00
"	10	" 10 Bbls. Apples	1.25		12	50
Feb.	2	" 4 Tons Hay	6.50		26	00
Dec.	28	" Cash to Balance			12	00
					57	50

The above is an account with James Brown, a Blacksmith, in which seven transactions are entered.

Transaction 1. January 2. James Brown shoes my horses, (each pupil may suppose them his,) for which I am to pay him $1.75. Here I am the receiver, and hence the debtor. He is the giver, and hence the creditor. I, then, having written his name in my book, credit him with the amount of the work done for me; but as the last two columns are understood to be for dollars and cents, it is not necessary to write the sign for dollars.

Tr. 2. Jan. 5. I sell James Brown 4 cords of hickory, for which he is to pay me $1.75 a cord. In this transaction he is the receiver, and hence the debtor, and I accordingly debit him for the amount, $7.00.

Tr. 3. Jan. 10. I sell James Brown 10 bbls. of apples at $1.25 a bbl., amounting to $12.50, and again debit him, as in 2d transaction.

Tr. 4. Feb. 2. I sell James Brown four tons of hay at $6.50 a ton, amounting to $26.00, and debit him accordingly, he having been the receiver, and hence the debtor, in the last three transactions.

Tr. 5. June 3. I buy of James Brown one lumber wagon, for which I am to pay him $50.00. Here he again becomes

How many transactions in the account with James Brown? What is the first transaction, and what the entry? What the second, and entry? The third, and entry? Fourth, and entry? Fifth, and entry?

1850						
Jan.	2	By	Shoeing Span of Horses		1	75
June	3	''	1 Lumber Wagon		50	00
Nov.	10	''	Repairing Sleigh		4	50
''	15	''	Shoeing Horse		1	25
					57	50

the giver and I the receiver, and I hence credit him accordingly.

Tr. 6. Nov. 10. James Brown repairs my sleigh, for which he charges me $4.50. In this transaction, as in the last, he is the giver, and I am the receiver, and I hence credit him with the amount of the work done.

Tr. 7. Nov. 15. Here James Brown shoes one of my horses, and the entry exhibits the necessary credit.

Settlement. Dec. 28. Accounts should be settled at least once every year. As, then, the end of the year approaches, I call on James Brown for my annual settlement with him. We first add the sums in the money columns of the credit side of the account, and find they amount to $57.50, which is the sum-total of all I have received from him. We next add the sums in the money columns of the debit side, and find they amount to $45.50, which is the sum-total of all I have let him have. We then subtract the amount of the debits from the amount of the credits. This gives a remainder of $12.00, which is the amount of my indebtedness to him. I pay him this sum, and debit him with "Cash to Balance." Finally, I draw single lines under the money columns, and after adding them and placing the amount, $57.50, under each, draw double lines beneath, to show that the account is balanced and closed.

Sixth, and entry? Seventh, and entry? How often should accounts be settled? How is this account settled and closed?

Samuel Adams *Dr.*

1850							
Jan.	10	To 75 *Bush. Wheat*		.80		60	00
"	15	" 80 " *Corn*		.40		32	00
Mar.	16	" 40 " *Potatoes*		.35		14	00
						106	00
		To *Balance brought down*				8	17

The foregoing is an account with Samuel Adams, a Retail Merchant. I have sold him produce at three different times, amounting in all to $106.00. Dec. 31.—I call on him for settlement. By adding the sums credited to him, we find they amount to $97.83. By subtracting this sum from the amount of his debits, it appears there is due me $8.17. As I have no occasion to use either money or goods at this time, and expect to do my trading with him another year, the account is balanced as follows: I credit him "By Balance," $8.17. This done, the debits and credits amount to the same. I now draw single lines under the money columns, directly opposite each other, as before, placing the amount under them, and drawing the double lines beneath to signify that the account is settled.

How is the account with Samuel Adams settled?

1850						
Jan.	4	By 25 lbs. Loaf Sugar	.13		3	25
"	10	" 2¼ Yds. Broadcloth	4.00		9	00
"	"	" 2¾ " Cassimere	2.00		5	50
"	"	" Trimmings for Coat and Vest			2	75
Feb.	4	" 21 Yds. Sheeting	.11		2	31
"	"	" 2 lbs. Saleratus	.07			14
"	"	" 1 " Black Tea				75
Apr.	12	" Bill of Crockery			12	56
"	"	" 30 Grain Bags	.25		7	50
"	"	" Bill of Goods for John Bruce			25	75
July	2	" my Order to John Bruce			22	50
Nov.	8	" 1 piece of Calico, 34 Yds.	.15		5	10
Dec.	14	" 8 lbs. Brown Sugar	.09			72
"	31	" Balance to new Acct.			8	17
					106	00

When one side of the account contains more entries than the other, as in this example, an oblique line should be drawn across the unoccupied space, as is here done. The amount of the debits and credits, when footed, should equal each other, and be on the same *horizontal* line.

The bill of goods on account of John Bruce, my hired man, bought April 12, I credit to the Merchant and debit to Bruce; also my order in his favor of July 2. When goods are credited by bill, the bill should be kept till the accounts are settled.

The sum credited "By Balance," on settlement, should be debited in the new account, under the same date, "To Balance," as in the example given.

When one side of the account contains more entries than the other, what rule should be observed in relation to the footings? What items that are debited in this account are credited in another account? When goods are credited by bill, how long should the bills be kept?

1850				
Apr.	12	To Bill of Goods from Sam. Adams	25	75
''	17	'' W. Wood for Making Clothes	7	50
July	2	'' my Order on Samuel Adams	22	50
Sept.	12	'' my Note at 60 days to Balance.	29	25
			85	00

Here is represented an account which John Bruce, my hired man: (for the terms of my contract with him, see Memorandum-book, 52d page.) The first and third *debits* in his account are *credits* in the account with Samuel Adams, as exhibited on the last preceding page. I have also debited him the amount paid W. Wood on his behalf for making a suit of clothes, and with my note to balance, and thus closed the account. I have debited him with my note, the same as I should have done with cash, had I paid him the money to balance. This fulfills my agreement with him, as per memorandum referred to. My note I shall of course expect to pay when it becomes due. (See Bills Payable, 45th page.)

These entries, and the two referred to in the account with Samuel Adams, are made in accordance with a principle already stated and elucidated, which enables us to determine where to enter every transaction belonging to personal accounts. The principle is this : The *receiver* is always the Dr., and the *giver* is always the Cr. No distinction is made between cash, promissory notes, goods, accepted orders, (see remarks in rela-

---

In case I make an order on Samuel Adams for $22.50, payable to John Bruce, how should I enter the transaction in their respective accounts? In case I give my note to John Bruce to balance an account on settlement, how do I enter the transaction in his account?

1850						
Apr.	12	By 3 Months Labor	10.00		30	00
Sept.	12	" 5 do. do.	11.00		55	00
					85	00

tion to Orders, on the 116th page,) money due for services, or houses and lands. Whenever a person *receives* any of these or other property from you, or you pay them *on his behalf*, the transaction should be entered on the debtor side of his account. When he pays them to you, or on your behalf, and thus becomes the *giver*, and you the receiver, the transaction should be entered on the credit side of his account. In the case of my order on Samuel Adams for $22.50 in favor of John Bruce, Adams is the giver, and hence the Cr.; and Bruce is the receiver, and hence the Dr. This principle is of universal application.

The symbol of a pair of scales on the title-page, which beautifully illustrates the general principle that the Dr. and Cr. sides of an account ought always to balance, particularly illustrates the account here introduced. As the four smaller weights at the left are exactly counterpoised by the two larger ones at the right, so the four smaller entries on the Dr. side of the account exactly balance the two larger ones on the Cr. side. Another symbol is referred to on the 121st page.

What general rule is stated which enables us to determine on which side of an account to enter a transaction? Does the rule apply to notes and orders as well as to money and goods? When a person receives property from you, or you pay it on his behalf, how is the transaction entered? How, when he pays to you or on your behalf? Is this principle of universal application? What principle does the symbol on the title-page illustrate? Apply that symbol to this account.

Wheatfield, 18 Acres Dr.

1849						
June	10	To 12 Days Plowing	2.00	24	00
"	20	" 4 do. Harrowing	1.50	6	00
Aug.	28	" 10 do. Plowing	2.00	20	00
Sept.	10	" 27 Bush. Seed Wheat	.80	21	60
"	"	" 2 Days Sowing	1.00	2	00
"	"	" 8 do. Harrowing	1.50	12	00
1850					
July	10	" Harvesting 18 Acres	1.50	27	00
Oct.	1	" Threshing 316 Bushels Wheat		22	20
"	13	" Marketing do. do.		6	00
"	"	" Int. on 18 Acres, $20 per Acre		25	20
"	"	" Profits on the Crop		70	20
				236	20

The above is an account with a Wheatfield of 18 acres, from which it appears that the net profits (after paying the interest on the value of the land, and all the expenses of raising the crop) are seventy dollars and twenty cents. The account is kept just as an account with a person is: The field is *debited* with every thing put upon it, with every expense made on its account, and with the interest on the land at a fair valuation. It is *credited* with every thing it produces, and with every thing received on its account. The excess of the credits over the debits gives the net profit, which must be entered on the Dr. side of the account in order to balance. Accounts may be kept in like manner with every branch of one's business, whether agricultural, mechanical, commercial, or speculative. If persons

In the account with a Wheatfield of 18 acres, what are the net profits? How is the account kept? With what is the field debited, and with what credited? How is the net profit ascertained? With what kinds of business may accounts be kept in this way?

1850						
Oct.	13	By 316 Bushels Wheat	.70	221	20
''	''	'' Straw for Fodder		15	00
				236	20

generally were to keep such accounts, they would thereby be enabled to ascertain, with great accuracy, what pursuits afford certain profits, and what particular department of their business is most lucrative; also, what enterprises are hazardous and unproductive; and, by regulating themselves accordingly, they would of course best promote their own pecuniary interests, and at the same time contribute most effectually to advance the general prosperity of the community in which they live.

When the debits in such an account exceed the credits, and it becomes necessary in balancing the account to make the last entry on the Cr. side, it is evident the enterprise is attended with *loss*, as is exemplified in the account with a Grain Speculator on the next folio.

What advantages would result to the individual and to the community if persons generally were to keep such accounts? When the debits in such an account exceed the credits, is the enterprise attended with *gain* or *loss*?

1850						
Nov.	10	To Cash for 10,000 Bush. Wheat	.72		7200	00
"	"	" Charges to Monroe per Bu.		.15	1500	00
1851						
Apr.	20	" do. at do. do.		.04	400	00
"	"	" Insurance against Fire ½ per cent.			43	50
"	27	" Lake Freight to Buffalo	.03		300	00
"	"	" Marine Insurance ½ per cent.			43	50
May	10	" Commis. for selling at Buffalo	.01		100	00
"	"	" Exchange on $8700 at ½ per cent.			43	50
"	"	" Interest on same for 6 mos.		.07	304	50
					9935	00

Above is the account of a Grain Speculator, who made a purchase the 10th of Nov., with the expectation of getting the same forward to Buffalo, making sales at 97 cents, and getting returns in two weeks. Had he realized his expectations he would have reduced the cost of the wheat to him in Buffalo, one cent per bushel of the charges in Monroe on account of storage for the winter, the insurance against fire, and 5½ months

1850						
Nov.	10	To Cash for 10,000 Bush. Wheat	.72		7200	00
"	"	" Charges to Monroe per Bu.		.15	1500	00
"	24	" do. at do. do.		.03	300	00
"	"	" Lake Freight and Marine Ins.			343	50
"	"	" Commission and Exchange			143	50
"	"	" Interest on $8700 for ½ month	.07		25	37
"	"	" Gain on the Speculation			187	63
/					9700	00

What was lost by a Grain Speculator in the Wheat Account here given?

1851						
May	5	By Proceeds of 4000 Bu. Wheat	.87½		3500	00
"	10	" do. 6000 do.	.87		5220	00
"	"	" Amount to Balance, (Loss)			1215	00
					9935	00

interest—amounting in all to   -   -   -   - $422.63

And his receipts would have been greater by   -   980.00

Making an actual difference in the result of   -   - $1402.63

Hoping to *gain* $187.63, as appears from his figuring below, he actually *lost* $1215.00, as appears from the account given above.

1850						
Nov.	25	By Returns on 10,000 Bu. Wheat .97			9700	00
					9700	00

NOTE.—In order to exhibit this account complete on one folio, the Lake freight and Marine insurance in the opposite entries, (which are the same as in the above account,) are combined; also the charges for Commission and Exchange.

What had he hoped to gain? What difference in result? How made up?

Cornfield, 8 Acres Dr.

1850						
Apr.	20	To ¼ of 56 Loads Manure	.25		3	50
May	1	" 3 Days Plowing	2.00		6	00
"	2	" 1 do. Harrowing			1	50
"	3	" 1½ do. Marking-out	1.50		2	25
"	5	" 1¼ Bu. Seed Corn	.50			63
"	"	" 4 Days Planting	.75		3	00
"	20	" 2 do. Cultivating	1.50		3	00
June	1	" 2 do. do.	1.50		3	00
"	15	" 2 do. Plowing	1.50		3	00
Sept.	10	" 5⅓ do. Cutting and Shocking	.75		4	00
Oct.	10	" Husking and Binding Stalks			20	00
".	"	" Putting into Cribs			8	00
1851						
Feb.	1	" Threshing 800 Bu. Corn	.01½		12	00
"	15	" Marketing do. do.	.01½		12	00
"	"	" Int. on 8 Acres at $20, $160	.07		11	20
"	"	" Profits on the Crop			255	92
					349	00

The profits on this crop of corn are very great, as is shown by the last entry in the debit side of the account; but then, the soil that produced it was very fruitful, and required but a small amount of labor in cultivation. Corn, moreover, usually requires twice hoeing; but this, which was raised on the River Raisin, in Monroe Co., Mich., was not hoed at all. It was "cultivated" between the rows, in one direction, the 20th of May, and in the other direction the 1st of June; and it was

Here is presented an account with a Crop of Corn of eight acres: What are the profits on the crop? How are this large yield and consequent profits accounted for? How was the field cultivated?

1850							
Oct.	10	By 10 Lds. Stalks, sold to J. B.	1.50		15	00
"	"	" 14 do. do. for Fodder	1.00		14	00
1851						
Feb.	15	" 800 Bushels Corn	.40		320	00
					349	00

plowed out once only, without hoeing, on the 15th of the latter month.

This crop was debited with only *one-fourth* the expense of manuring, because the land was permanently enriched, and the benefit will probably be realized in the next three crops to as great an extent as in this. It is hence apparent that but one-fourth of the expense of enriching should be debited to this crop.

Why was not this crop of corn debited with the whole expense of enriching the field ?

2*

1851								
Jan.	1	To Cash on hand					14	50
''	4	'' rec'd for	4	Cords Wood	1.50		6	00
''	10	'' '' ''	10	bbls. Apples	2.00		20	00
''	15	'' '' ''	14	Cords Wood	1.50		21	00
''	23	'' '' ''	2	bbls. Pork	9.00		18	00
							79	50
Jan.	31	To Balance brought down					38	67

An account may and should be kept with Cash, the same as with an individual, as in the above example. Persons who have a limited cash deal may keep their cash account in the Ledger, and in the same manner they do their personal accounts. But when one's cash account is extensive, or the entries in it become frequent and numerous, it will be best to keep the account in a separate Cash-book provided for that purpose, which should be balanced at the close of each day. In opening the account, Cash should be debited with the amount on hand. All moneys *received* should be entered on the Dr. side of the Cash account, and all moneys *paid out*, on the Cr. side of the account. In balancing the account, Cash should be credited with the amount on hand. The amount on hand at the opening of an account with Cash, together with the sums *received* at different times, should exactly equal the amount of the sums *paid out* and the cash on hand at the time of settlement.

How may an account be kept with Cash? When may the Cash account be kept in the Ledger? When should a separate Cash-book be provided? With what should Cash be debited on opening the account? What entries are made on the Dr., and what on the Cr. side of the account? What credit should be made in balancing the account? What amounts should be equal?

1851						
Jan.	3	By Paid for 1 pr. Buckskin Mittens				63
"	7	" " " 10 lbs. Brown Sugar .07				70
"	10	" " " Books as per Bill			7	50
"	17	" " Subscription for Preaching			18	00
"	24	" " 1 qr's tuition for 2 sch's 7.00			14	00
"	31	" Balance on hand			38	67
					79	50

The first entry in the Cash account must always be on the Dr. side, for no person can pay out money unless he first has it on hand. It is likewise apparent that the credit entries in the Cash account can never exceed the amount of the debit entries. When these are exactly equal, there can be no Cash on hand. When the Dr. side of the account amounts to more than the Cr. side, the difference, if the account has been correctly kept, will equal the Cash on hand.

An account may be balanced and continued on the same page, or two accounts may be kept on the same folio, as in the following examples, according to circumstances. Whenever a folio is filled, and the account not closed, the two sides of the account should be added and the amount carried to some other folio designated. (See example on the next folio.)

Where must the first entry be made in the Cash account? Why? Can the credit entries ever exceed the debit entries? When the Dr. side amounts to more than the Cr. side, what should the difference be equal to? When an account is settled, may it be reopened on the same page? May two accounts be kept on the same folio? When a folio is filled and the account not closed, what should be done?

John Martin   Dr.

1849						
Jan.	10	To	10 lbs. Butter	.15	1	50
Feb.	4	"	12 " do.	15	1	80
"	"	"	15 Bu. Corn	.40	6	00
July	2	"	20 Yds. Tow Cloth	.34	6	80
Nov.	30	"	40 Bu. Wheat	.80	32	00
1850						
Jan.	1	"	Balance to new acct.		4	72
					52	82
1850						
Jan.	10	To	8 Bu. Potatoes	.40	3	20
Apr.	4	"	6 " do.	.44	2	64
Nov.	25	"	80 " Wheat	.78	62	40
"	26	"	45 " Corn	.35	15	75
					83	99

Henry Van Allen   Dr.

1850						
Jan.	6	To	2¼ Yds. Broadcloth for self	4.00	9	00
"	"	"	2½ Yds. Cassimere for Pants.	2.30	5	75
"	"	"	Trimmings for Suit Clothes		4	25
Feb.	4	"	40 lbs. Brown Sugar per Wife	.08	3	20
"	"	"	1 Piece Sheeting, 30½ Yds.	.10	3	05
"	"	"	10 Yds. M. De Laine	.34	3	40
"	"	"	Trimmings			31
Apr.	9	"	4 Yds. Irish Linen	.56	2	24
"	"	"	1½ " Linen Edging	.20		30
					31	50

Carried to folio 9

John Martin   Cr.⁸

1849						
Jan.	10	By 6 lbs. Brown Sugar	.08			48
Feb.	4	" 10 Yds. Calico, by Julia	.17		1	70
"	"	" Bill of Crockery			6	50
July	2	" Cash advanced on Wheat			40	00
"	"	" 1 Piece of Sheeting, 31 Yds.	.10		3	10
Nov.	30	" 10 lbs. Nails, by John	.06			60
"	"	" 1 Currycomb, do.				44
					52	82
1850						
Jan.	1	By Balance brought down			4	72
Apr.	4	" 1 Piece Shirting, 32 Yds.	.09		2	88
May	1	" 2 Hoes for John and George	.88		1	76
Dec.	26	" Cash to Balance			74	63
					83	99

Henry Van Allen   Cr.

1850						
Jan.	10	By 20 Bushels of Wheat	.75		15	00

See this account at the 67th page,
kept by the *Second Form.*

| | | | | | 15 | 00 |

Carried to folio 9

37

1850						
May	10	To amount from folio 8			31	50
"	15	" 2 Linen Hdkfs. per Jane	.37½			75
"	"	" 16 Yds. Watered Silk	1.25		20	00
"	"	" 1 Pr. Kid Buskins			1	25
July	1	" Piece Shirting, 30 Yds.	.11		3	30
"	"	" 14 lbs. Loaf Sugar	.14		1	96
Aug.	4	" 2 Palm Leaf Hats	.31¼			63
"	10	" 10 Yds. Brown Linen	.35		3	50
"	"	" 24 " Linen Gingham	.31		7	44
Oct.	"	" 4 " Broadcloth	3.00		12	00
"	"	" 1⅛ doz. Buttons	.25			29
"	"	" Trimmings as per Bill			12	25
					94	87

This account is here continued from the preceding folio. It might have been carried to any other, as well as brought here, by making the proper entry at the foot of the page from which it is carried, showing the folio upon which it is continued.

The books of the Creditor should specify every item sold. This is always important, and especially so when the entries are of considerable amount. The last entry on the Dr. side of this account with H. Van Allen is hence *radically defective*, not a single article debited being specified. The bill, if purchased by any other person than himself, may never reach him; or if it does, it may be mislaid, and in the settlement it may be impossible to satisfy him that this amount has ever been received by him or on his account. The Debtor may *give credit* for goods as per bill received, if he chooses to do so, as in the case of a "bill of crockery" in the account with John Martin on the last

---

What should the books of the Creditor specify? What of the last Dr. entry in the account with H. Van Allen? May the Debtor give credit in his books per bill received? In such cases what should be done with the bill?

Henry Van Allen   Cr.

1850						
Jan.	10	By amount from folio 8		15	00
Oct.	15	" 90 Bushels Wheat	.87	78	30
Dec.	29	" Cash to Balance		1	57
		See this account at the 67th page, kept by the *Second Form*.		94	87

folio, and as is twice done in the account with Samuel Adams—once for a " bill of crockery," and once for a " bill of goods for John Bruce." But even in such cases, to prevent any occasion for difficulty, it is best to preserve the bills until the accounts are settled.

If on the Dr. side of my account with a person, I enter " To bill of goods," and carry out only the amount, he may not give me any credit at all, and on settlement he may dispute the account, and I may then be unable to specify a single article sold him. On the contrary, if I enter on the credit side of my ac count with a person, " By bill of goods," and give the amount, I thereby acknowledge the receipt of the *amount ;* but in case the books do not exactly agree, difficulties may still arise in the settlement, if the bill is not preserved so as to compare items. The following rule should be observed :

Why should the items sold be specified in the books of the Creditor, when they may be entered per bill in the books of the Debtor ? What rule is given for making Dr. and Cr. entries ?

RULE FOR DR. AND CR. ENTRIES.

The books of the Creditor should specify both the quantity and the value of every article debited. The books of the Debtor should likewise specify both the quantity and the value of every article credited, unless *bills* are received of the goods or wares purchased, *which is always preferable.* When bills are given, the holder of them may enter the *amount only* in his account, but he should keep the bills on file until settlement.

BILLS OF PURCHASE.

A Bill of Purchase is a statement of goods or wares bought at one time, embracing both the quantity and the price of each article, and the amount of the whole. If paid at the time of purchase, it should be receipted by the seller, as in the first example on the opposite page; if settled "by note," as in the second example; and if "charged in account," as in the third.

When a bill of goods is paid for at the time they are purchased, it is sufficient for each party to enter the transaction in his Cash account, unless there is a personal account between them, in which case the goods should be debited, and the money credited, in the books of the seller; but in the books of the purchaser, the goods should be credited, and the money debited. When payment is made "by note," the seller should make the necessary entry under the head of Bills Receivable, and the purchaser under the head of Bills Payable, which is all that is necessary unless there is a personal account between the parties, in which case the whole transaction should be shown, as though money had been paid instead of a note given; but

When a bill of goods is "charged in account," the seller should simply debit the purchaser with the items sold, which should be credited in the books of the latter.

What is a bill of purchase? When a bill of goods is paid for at the time of purchase, what entries should be made in the books of each party? When payment is made "by note," what entries should be made? When a bill of goods is "charged in account," what entries should the parties make in their books?

Monroe, July 10, 1851.

James Henry,

Bought of C. G. Johnson,

24 Seamless Bags, at	.31	7.44
20 lbs. of Brown Sugar	.07	1.40
14 " Rice	.05	.70
1 " Black Tea		.75

Received Payment, $10.29

C. G. Johnson,

Per C. Luce.

Monroe, August 12, 1851

Henry Hubbard,

Bought of Isaac Merrill,

1 Pair of pegged Kip Boots	3.75
1 " Kid Buskins, for Wife	1.25
1 " " " for Daughter	1.00

Rec'd Payment by Note at 30 days, $6.00

Isaac Merrill.

Monroe, September 10, 1851.

David Bronson,

Bought of Miller & Son,

10 lbs. Brown Sugar	.08	.80
16 Yds. Calico	.20	3.20

Charged in Account, $4.00

Miller & Son.

Per Richardson.

BILLS OF ACCOUNT.

A BILL OF ACCOUNT, called also an Account Current, is a record of the unsettled transactions between the parties named in the account, comprising both debits and credits. It should contain a list of the items bought and sold, together with their prices, and should show the date of each transaction; thus:

George Graham,

In acct. with James Armitage, Dr.

1850							
Jan.	10	To 3 Gallons Molasses .50	1	50			
//	//	// 2 Sets Cups and Saucers		50			
Feb.	4	// 15 Yds. Calico .15	2	25			
//	//	// 2½ // Flannel .20		50			
//	//	// 3 Papers of Pins .10		30			
May	10	// 4 lbs. Coffee .13		52			
//	//	// 12 lbs. Brown Sugar .09	1	08	6	65	
1850		———— Cr. ————					
Feb.	4	By 10 lbs. Butter .14	1	40			
May	10	// Cash, per son George	1	60			
//	//	// Balance Due	3	65	6	65	

EXAMPLES FOR PRACTICE.

In the following examples, where several articles of the same kind are bought or sold, the price and the quantity are given, and the pupil is left to carry out the amount. If the computations are correctly made, the accounts will exactly balance.

What is a bill of account? What should it contain and show?

James Farmer,
    In Acct. with Ira Merchant,   *Dr.*

1851								
Jan.	10	To 3½ Yds. Flannel	.50					
"	"	" 6 " Calico	.15					
"	"	" 7¾ " Shirting	.16					
May	4	" 1 Hoe, per son John			88			
June	10	" 2 Scythes and Snaths		3	50	8	27

1851		Cr.						
Jan.	10	By 9 Bushels Oats	.23					
May	4	" 4 Doz. Hens' Eggs	.09					
June	16	" 8 " do.	.08					
July	1	" Cash to Balance		5	20	8	27

Isaac Paywell,
    In Acct. with Ira Merchant,   *Cr.*

1851								
Feb.	12	By 40 Bushels Oats	.27					
"	"	" 12 do. Corn	.44					
"	15	" 60 do. Wheat	.84			66	48

1851		Dr.						
Mar.	10	To 4 Yds. Broadcloth	4.50					
"	"	" 16 " Black Silk	1.00					
"	"	" Cash to Balance		32	48	66	48

In the last example, the credits occurring before and exceeding the debits are placed first in the account. Both examples
are differently arranged under the Second Form of Accounts.

Bills Receivable.

When made.		Maker's Name.	Payee's Name.
1850			
June	10	Samuel Ware	J. M., or Order
"	15	Jno. N. Isham	J. B., or Bearer
July	1	Thomas Payne	H. W., or Order
"	12	A. H. Murray	The Bearer
Aug.	1	James Darrow	Ira Mayhew

Bills Payable.

When made.		Maker's Name.	Payee's Name.
1850			
Sept.	12	Ira Mayhew	John Bruce
1851			
June	10	"	Jno. Owen
July	1	"	"
"	15	"	Treas. Miss. Soc.

The term BILLS RECEIVABLE includes all written obligations for the payment of money which one holds against other persons, such as Promissory Notes, Due Bills, Orders, Drafts, etc. When any of these are received by you, they should be at once entered under the head, Bills Receivable, after which they may be placed on their proper files. Then, by referring to this title, it will be easy to see when any obligation you hold becomes due, where payable, etc., and thus save yourself the trouble of examining various packages of papers, the contents of which are here noted. Persons engaged in extensive business find it convenient to keep separate Bill-books; but those who transact a limited business will not require more than a folio of their Ledger, properly ruled.

What are Bills Receivable? Where should they be entered when received, and why? When are separate Bill-books necessary?

Bills Receivable.

Where Payable.	When due.		Amount.		Remarks.
	1850				
Mich. St. Bank	July	10	75	50	Cashed June 12
	1851				
	Jan.	15	24	75	Pd. Dec. 10, 1850
At Maker's Store	"	1	60	00	Pd. at Maturity
	July	12	17	14	Pd. July 10, $10
At my House	Dec.	30	25	00	

Bills Payable.

Where Payable.	When due.		Amount.		Remarks.
	1850				
At my Residence	Nov.	12	29	25	Pd. at Maturity
	1851				
At Owen's, Detroit	June	25	10	50	Pd. June 20, 1851
" "	July	15	20	00	Pd. at Maturity
	Nov.	15	40	84	

The term BILLS PAYABLE includes all written obligations for the payment of money, of whatever kind, given by one to other persons. Whenever you give such an obligation you should enter the particulars under this head. It is of the utmost importance to note, at the time, at least the *amount* and *when due*, together with the *payee's name* and *where payable*.

The *maker* of a note, (called also the giver or drawer,) is the person who gives the note, and who must sign it. The *payee* of a note is the person to whom it is made payable. The place where a note is payable should always be specified whenever the *payee*, (or holder of the note at the time it becomes due,) does not expect to call at the *maker's* place of residence.

What are Bills Payable? Where should they be entered when given? What should be especially noted? Who is the *maker* of a note? Who the *payee*? When should the place where a note is payable be specified?

Bills Receivable Dr.

1850							
June	10	To note against Samuel Ware			75	50
"	15	" do. do. Jno. N. Isham			24	75
July	1	" do. do. Thomas Payne			60	00
"	12	" do. do. A. H. Murray			17	14
Aug.	1	,, do. do. James Darrow			25	00
					202	39
1851						
Dec.	1	To Balance brought down			32	14

Bills Payable Dr.

1850					
Sept.	12	To note to John Bruce, at 60 days		29	25
1851					
June	10	" do. J. Owen, payable in Detroit		10	50
July	1	" do. do. do. do.		20	00
"	15	" do. Treas. Miss. Society		40	84
				100	59
Dec.	1	To balance brought down		40	84

In connection with the general statement concerning Bills Payable and Bills Receivable, presented on the last preceding folio, it will often be found convenient to keep a debtor and credit account with each, in the same manner that an account with an individual, with any branch of business, or with cash, is kept. Such an account is exhibited on this folio, based upon the same transactions that are recorded upon the preceding folio. The entry made in each, under date Nov. 12, 1850, re-

How may a Dr. and Cr. account be kept with Bills Receivable and Bills Payable? Upon what transactions is the account here presented based?

Bills Receivable   Cr.

1850					
June	12	By Cash on S. Ware's Note		75	50
Dec.	10	" do. on J. N. Isham's Note		24	75
1851					
Jan.	1	" do. of T. Payne on his Note		60	00
July	10	" do. of A. H. Murray		10	00
Dec.	1	" Balance due		32	14
				202	39

Bills Payable   Cr.

1850					
Nov.	12	By Cash to John Bruce, in full		29	25
1851					
June	20	" Note taken up at J. Owen's		10	50
July	15	" do. do. do.		20	00
Dec.	1	" Balance, (not due)		40	84
				100	59

lates to a note given John Bruce in the settlement of our personal account, recorded on the 26th page.

A person keeping a debtor and credit account with Bills Receivable and Bills Payable can, by periodically balancing these accounts, ascertain what amount remains unpaid on the obligations *he holds against others*, and whether this sum is increasing or lessening from time to time; also, *his own indebtedness* on account of notes and other bills payable, and whether it is increasing or diminishing in amount.

What can a person keeping such an account at any time ascertain?

GENERAL SETTLEMENT.

A General Settlement shows how a person stands with the world, or with all persons with whom he transacts business, taken collectively. It is made by taking an inventory of one's property, to the fair value of which he must add the *sum of the balances due him* from others in the settlement of his *personal accounts*, and the balance due him on *bills receivable*. From the total amount of these he must deduct the *sum of the balances due others* in the settlement of his personal accounts, together with the balance that may become due from him on *bills payable*. The difference of these amounts will evidently represent his exact standing with the world.

Such general settlements should be made at the end of each year, immediately after one's annual settlements take place. By comparing the result of each general settlement with those of preceding ones, persons can readily see how much they have gained or lost during the past year, or in any given number of years. But without such a general settlement it is impossible for persons engaged in an extensive debit and credit business, (constantly exchanging goods and wares for bills receivable that are liquidated from time to time, and frequently issuing and cancelling bills payable,) to possess any definite knowledge of their exact standing with the world. No one, then, who has any adequate regard for his own pecuniary interests, and for his reputation as a business man, should fail to make such a settlement at the close of every year's business. In the light of such facts as would thus be thrown upon one's business, ultimate success is almost certain ; while, if left to grope his way as it

---

What does a General Settlement show ? How is a General Settlement made ? When should such a settlement be made? How can persons ascertain what they have gained or lost during the past year, or in any number of years? Can persons possess any definite knowledge of their standing with the world without such general settlements? What is said of such settlements in connection with one's *success* or *failure* in business?

were in the dark, he not only jeopards success, but even courts a failure.

When one's indebtedness exceeds what he possesses and what is due him, taken together, he is said to be *worse than nothing*.

MEMORANDUM-BOOK.

This book, whose name indicates its general character, is second in importance to the Ledger only. In it should be entered every thing of importance relating to a person's business that does not properly belong to the Ledger. It will often contain agreements, the carrying out of which will require frequent entries in the Ledger, as is illustrated in the case of John Bruce, whose account has already been given at the 26th page. A memorandum of my agreement with him is given in the following Memorandum-book, under date Jan. 12th, 1850.

The Memorandum-book should commence with a general inventory of one's property. It should contain memorandums of agreements and of contracts of various kinds. It should not only contain a general statement of one's business affairs, but in it every important particular relating to his business which he ought himself to remember, or which should be known to his representatives, should be carefully recorded. All business engagements of importance which you make, to be fulfilled hereafter, should be carefully recorded in this book at the time they are entered into; and when they are met, a brief entry should be made in the space left at the right, stating the facts. Where the engagement is simple, as in the case of my contract with Dr. J. Goodman, made March 16th, and promptly fulfilled, it is not necessary to open a personal account with him in the

---

When is a person said to be *worse than nothing*? What is said of the importance of the Memorandum-book? What should be entered in it? With what should this book commence? When should engagements be recorded? When met, what entry should be made? When may the entries relating to an agreement be made in the Cash-book only, and when should they be made in one's personal account?

Ledger. It is sufficient to debit Cash with the amount received of him. But in case the contract is more complex, and requires several entries to be made at different times, as is exemplified in my agreement with Jacob Merchant, made Nov. 10th, it becomes necessary to open a personal account with him in the Ledger, where all transactions relating to the contract should be faithfully entered.

Agreements should generally be made in writing, and especially when much time is to elapse before their fulfillment, or they are in any degree complex. When this is not practicable it may be well to make the agreement in the presence of witnesses, as in case of the engagement to furnish wood, entered into Dec. 1st. In such cases the memorandum should be made as soon after the agreement as practicable, while all the particulars are fresh in the memory.

The Memorandum-book should be frequently reviewed to see what contracts, if any, remain to be fulfilled, when the proper entries should be made opposite such as have been performed. In cases like that entered under date Dec. 4th, the reserved space may be filled at the time the entry is made. It will generally be advisable, and especially in case your circumstances are much changed, to make out a general inventory of your property at the commencement of each year. In case of a limited business, the Memorandum-book, like the Cash-book and Bill-book, may be kept in the Ledger, but it will generally be preferable to keep it in a separate book, after the manner of the one hereto annexed.*

---

* The form of Memorandum-book, exhibited on the three following pages, although original with the author of this treatise, was first presented to the public as part of a regular system of Book-keeping, in a recent work by P. MacGregor, Esq., of New York, in which the subject is treated at greater length.

When should agreements be made in writing? When not in writing, how may they be made? Why should the Memorandum-book be frequently reviewed? How often should a general inventory be made? How should the Memorandum-book be kept?

GENERAL INVENTORY OF MY PROPERTY.

January 1st, 1850.

Value of Farm, including Buildings and Fixtures - - - -	4400.00
Value of Timber Lot - - -	850.00
do. Teams and Agricultural Implements - - - - - -	475.00
Stock of Cattle - - - - -	875.00
do. Sheep - - - - -	500.00
Cash on hand - - - - -	80.75
Note against Peter York - -	84.00
do. do. Ira Butts - - -	15.75
Wm. Williams owes me on Acct.	84.00
Oren Olds do. do.	15.00
Total Value of Property - -	$7379.50

I Owe as Follows:

On Timber Lot - -	150.00	
J. Olds on Note - -	14.75	
H. Brown on Acct. -	12.50	
O. Hyde do. -	2.25	179.50
Net Capital this Day		$7200.00

The increase of my property since Jan. 1st, 1849, has been $450.81.

My business is in a more prosperous state than ever before, for which I have great reason to be thankful.

———————— *4th.* ————————

Engaged to furnish J. Bronson with Butter for his family's use till May 1st, for 15 cents a pound, to be paid for in cash as delivered.

May 1st, engagement fulfilled and new one made this day.

———————— *6th.* ————————

Commenced trading with H. Van Allen, who is to take my Wheat at cash price when delivered; likewise the crop now on the ground. For particulars see written agreement.

Contract fulfilled and account settled, Dec. 29th, 1850.

January 12*th*, 1850.

John Bruce commenced work on farm this day, for 8 months, on conditions fully set forth in our written contract. For the first three months I am to give him $10 per month, and for the remaining 5 months $11 per month. I am to give him what store pay he wants, from time to time, never exceeding his earnings, and to give him my note on settlement for any balance that may remain due, payable by the middle of November next.

Settled Sept. 12th, and gave my note to balance for $29.25, at sixty days. Paid note Nov. 12th. Bruce wishes to work for me next season

———— *Mar.* 16*th.* ————

Engaged to furnish Dr. J. Goodman with 95 pounds of Maple Sugar, to be accounted for on delivery at 12 cents per pound.

All settled, April 20th.

———— *April* 15*th.* ————

Agreed with James Underhill to plant sixteen-acre lot (No. 7) to corn, on conditions fully set forth in contract this day made.

All obligations performed, Nov. 10th, 1850.

———— *May* 1*st.* ————

Contracted to supply J. Bronson with Butter for family use till Oct. 1st, at 12 cents per pound. I have also agreed to let him have all the Cheese from my dairy, as the same shall become merchantable, to be paid for on delivery, at $6 per 100 lbs.

All obligations performed, Nov. 1st, 1850.

———— 14*th.* ————

Engaged to put sixteen tons of hay, well cured and in good condition, into Stephen Wakeland's barn by the 15th of July, to be paid for 1st Sept. at $7.25 per ton.

Engagements all discharged, Sept. 1st, 1850.

June 7th, 1850.

Employed Harriet Benson to do house-work for 13 weeks, at $1.25 per week.

Wages paid, Oct. 10th.

———— *Sept. 15th.* ————

Harriet Ann has this day entered upon her duties as First Assistant in the Union School, at $15 per month, or $45 per quarter of twelve weeks.

Wages paid, Dec. 20th.

———— " ————

Henry and Frances have this day commenced attending the Union School for the winter.

They left school March 1st, 1851.

———— *Nov. 10th.* ————

Purchased groceries for the winter of Jacob Merchant, to whom I have contracted 800 bushels of corn at 40 cents per bushel, the balance not traded out to be paid for in cash when the full amount is delivered.

All engagements discharged, November 20th.

———— *Dec. 1st.* ————

Engaged to furnish Ira Wilson with 20 cords of Hickory, at $1.50 a cord, to be delivered at his house by the 15th of January, and to be paid for by the 10th of April. Present, Hiram Wilson and Jacob Townsend.

Obligations all discharged, May 1st, 1851.

———— *4th.* ————

Mill-dam carried away by a freshet, and mill much injured.

Loss $140.00.

53

EXAMPLES FOR PRACTICE.

FIRST FORM OF ACCOUNTS.

The following examples are introduced, the better to enable the pupil to reduce to practice the knowledge of Book-keeping which he has already acquired. Each example consists of several transactions with the same individual, which, taken together, constitute a separate account, that should be opened, conducted, and closed, as in the case of examples already given.

For this purpose the pupil may at first rule the necessary quantity of separate sheets of paper, according to the instructions given at the 19th page. If the computations are correctly made, and the transactions are rightly entered, the last entry in the account will agree with the answer given after the last transaction in each example.

After each example has been solved, and the account has been accurately made out and properly balanced, the pupil will do well to copy his work neatly into the Account-book which has been prepared to accompany this volume, or into some other suitable one provided for that purpose.

EXAMPLE I.

This example consists of a series of transactions between the Book-keeper (each pupil may suppose himself or herself the person) and Asa P. Leonard, a country merchant.

NOTE TO TEACHERS.—The teacher should stimulate his pupils to make vigorous efforts to solve all of the "Examples for Practice," without consulting the Key for aid. When examples have been correctly solved, as an *encouragement* the pupil may with propriety be allowed to compare his work with that in the Key, but rarely (if at all) for the purpose of detecting mistakes.

Why are examples for practice introduced into this work? Of what does each example consist, and how should it be treated? What suggestion is given for the pupil? How may you know whether the computations are correctly made, and the transactions rightly entered? What suggestion is made in relation to the use of an Account-book? Of what does the first example given in the first form of accounts consist? What may each pupil suppose himself?

Transaction 1. Jan. 4, 1850. Sold Asa P. Leonard one quarter of Beef, weighing 150 lbs. for five cents a pound. Received in partial payment 2 lbs. of Black Tea, at 70 cents a pound; 4 lbs. of Coffee at 14 cents a pound; and 25 lbs. of Brown Sugar at 10 cents a pound.

Tr. 2. Jan. 25. Bought three gallons of Molasses at forty-four cents a gallon.

Tr. 3. Feb. 10. Sold 40 lbs. of Pork worth eight cents a pound. Received forty dollars in Cash.

Tr. 4. Feb. 15. Sold fourteen bushels of Corn for forty-five cents a bushel.

Tr. 5. May 10. Plowed his Garden, for which I am to receive one dollar and seventy-five cents.

Tr. 6. May 15. Sold eighteen bushels of Potatoes for thirty-five cents a bushel.

Tr. 7. June 12. Sold 250 lbs. of Wool at forty cents a pound. Received 18 yards of Calico at 15 cents a yard, and three papers of pins at five cents each.

Tr. 8. July 12. Have done two days' Work with Team, for which I am to receive one dollar and seventy-five cents a day.

Tr. 9. Nov. 1. I have pastured his cow for fourteen weeks, for which I am to receive 20 cents a week.

Tr. 10. Dec. 4. I have this day finished drawing him twenty-four cords of Beech and Maple, for which I am to receive one dollar and fifty cents a cord. I have bought of him one pair of Kip Brogans for $1.25; 18 lbs. of Rice at six cents a pound; 9 lbs. Loaf Sugar at fourteen cents a pound; and 9 yards of Merrimack Sheeting at 9 cents a yard.

Tr. 11. Dec. 29. I have this day settled with him and received the balance due me in Cash. What was the last credit entry? *Ans.* $114.32.

NOTE.—The solution of this example is given on the 6th and 7th pages of the Key. To find the solution of any other example, look, as in this case, immediately under the title of the account, in the Key, for the page or pages upon which the example is recorded in the Book-keeping, which are there given in the same type with this note

EXAMPLE II.

This example consists of a series of transactions with O. D. Knowlton, a saddle and harness maker.

Transaction 1. Jan. 4, 1851. Sold O. D. Knowlton eight bushels of Potatoes at thirty-five cents a bushel, and four bushels of Corn at forty-two cents a bushel.

Tr. 2. Feb. 10. Sold him ten bushels of Potatoes for thirty-five cents a bushel, and twelve bushels of Wheat at eighty cents a bushel.

Tr. 3. May 1. Sold him sixteen pounds of Butter at twelve and a half cents a pound. Bought of him one set of Double Harness, valued at thirty dollars.

Tr. 4. May 6. Sold him fourteen bushels of Corn for forty-five cents a bushel.

Tr. 5. June 10. Sold him four bushels of Potatoes at thirty-five cents a bushel. Also, bought of him one Brass Plated Single Harness, valued at thirty-five dollars.

Tr. 6. July 2. Bought one Saddle, Bridle, and Martingale, the whole valued at eighteen dollars and fifty cents.

Tr. 7. July 10. Sold him ten tons of Hay valued at four dollars and twenty-five cents a ton.

Tr. 8. Sept. 25. I have pastured four Cows for him ten weeks, for which I am to receive twenty cents a week for each Cow; also, one Horse nine weeks, for twenty-five cents a week. We this day settle, and I pay him the balance due in Cash. How much do I pay him?   *Ans.* $3.47.

EXAMPLE III.

This example consists of a series of transactions with Isaac Mitchell, who keeps a boot and shoe store.

Transaction 1. Jan. 1, 1851. Bought of Isaac Mitchell

one pair of Kip Boots for three dollars, and one pair of Buffalo Over-shoes for two dollars and fifty cents.

Tr. 2. Jan. 10. Sold him two dozen Hens' Eggs at fourteen cents a doz.

Tr. 3. Feb. 10. Sold him four pounds of Butter at fifteen cents a pound, and two bushels of Wheat at seventy-five cents a bushel. Also, bought of him one pair of India Rubber Overshoes for one dollar and twenty-five cents, and one pair of Buckskin Mittens for seventy-five cents.

Tr. 4. March 4. Sold him one quarter of Beef weighing one hundred and seventy-five pounds for five cents a pound. Also, bought of him one pair of Congress Gaiters for three dollars; two pair of Misses' Gaiters at one dollar and twenty-five cents each; and two pair of Children's Gloves at fifteen cents a pair.

Tr. 5. May 14. Sold him eighteen pounds of Wool for thirty cents a pound, and fourteen pounds of Butter at eleven cents a pound. Bought two pair of R. R. Jenny Linds at one dollar and twenty-five cents a pair; one pair of Enamel Gaiters for two dollars and fifty cents; and six Linen Handkerchiefs at sixty cents each.

Tr. 6. June 5. Bought two pair of Boys' Suspenders at fifteen cents a pair, and three pair of Mixed Half Hose at twenty cents a pair.

Tr. 7. June 10. Bought one Leghorn Hat for one dollar and fifty cents; two pair of Calf Buskins for one dollar a pair; and three pair Black Cotton Hose at twenty-five cents a pair. Also, settled the account and paid the amount due. What was it? *Ans.* $8.98.

EXAMPLE IV.

This example exhibits a Sheep and Wool Account. In this account the cost of the sheep, and every thing paid out on their account, should be entered on the Dr. side. On the Cr. side of the account should be entered every thing that is received on account of the sheep ; as wool, surviving sheep, and lambs.

Transaction 1. June 1, 1850. Bought one hundred and sixty Sheep at one dollar and twenty-five cents a head.

Tr. 2. Dec. 15. The Sheep have been in pasture since their purchase for six and one half months. Pasturing is worth three dollars a month for one hundred Sheep, and at the same rate for any greater number.

Tr. 3. March 15, 1851. The Sheep have been fed on hay for three months. Foddering is estimated worth twelve dollars a month for one hundred Sheep, and at the same rate for a greater number.

Tr. 4. June 1. The Sheep have been in pasture since March 15th, at the rates specified in the second transaction. Paid for washing and shearing six dollars per one hundred Sheep.* Cut from them six hundred pounds of Wool worth forty cents a pound. There are one hundred and fifty-two old Sheep living, worth one dollar and twenty-five cents a head, and sixty-four Lambs worth seventy-five cents each. What must be entered on the Dr. side in closing the account, as profits on one hundred and sixty Sheep for one year? *Ans.* $153.60.

EXAMPLE V.

The fifth and sixth examples consist of a series of transactions with Henry Webster, a bookseller and stationer. The account, which was settled July 10th, was reopened the 10th of September. If the sixth example is entered on the same folio with the fifth, the name of Henry Webster need not be written the

---

* This account should, under this date, be debited with the interest on the cost of one hundred and sixty sheep at seven per cent.

What should be entered on the Dr. side of this account? What on the Cr. side? Of what do the fifth and sixth examples consist?

second time, but the account may be reopened, after the manner of the continuation of the account with John Martin, as given at the 36th and 37th pages.

Transaction 1. Jan. 1, 1850. Sold Henry Webster fifteen and one half pounds of Butter for fourteen cents a pound, and twenty-five pounds of Cheese at eight cents a pound. Bought of him one Family Bible worth three dollars; one Webster's Dictionary worth three dollars and fifty cents; and one copy of Mayhew on Popular Education for one dollar.

Tr. 2. Jan. 5. Sold him forty pounds of Butter at fourteen cents a pound.

Tr. 3. Jan. 10. Bought one Thomson's Higher Arithmetic for seventy-five cents; one Smith's New Arithmetic for fifty cents; and two copies of Tower's Intellectual Algebra, at thirty-seven and a half cents each.

Tr. 4. June 4. Sold him ten pounds of Linen Rags at four cents a pound. Bought of him four quires of Writing Paper at twenty cents a quire; two Tower's Gradual Reader at twenty-five cents each; and two copies of Cobb's Spelling Book, at ten cents each.

Tr. 5. July 1. Sold him ten pounds of Butter at ten cents a pound, and four dozen Hens' Eggs at eight cents a dozen. Bought one Wells' Grammar at thirty-eight cents, and two copies of Thomson's Practical Arithmetic at thirty-eight cents each.

Tr. 6. July 10. Settled and paid the amount due in cash. How much was it? *Ans.* $0.65.

EXAMPLE VI.

This example consists of a series of transactions with Henry Webster, the bookseller and stationer named in the last preceding example.

If the account with an individual is settled and balanced, and subsequently reopened on the same folio, is it necessary to write his name the second time?

Transaction 1. Sept. 10, 1850. Sold him twenty-five bushels of Potatoes at thirty cents a bushel, and ten pounds of Butter at twelve and a half cents a pound. Bought of him two quires of Writing Paper at twenty-five cents each; one Ackerman's Natural History for fifty cents; and one Day-book and one Ledger, each containing five quires of paper, at thirty-four cents a quire.

Tr. 2. Nov. 1. Bought of him one Thomson's Higher Arithmetic, one Davies' University Arithmetic, and one Perkins' Higher Arithmetic, at seventy-five cents each.

Tr. 3. Nov. 10. Bought of him one Smith's Quarto Geography for seventy-five cents, and two copies of Guernsey's History of the United States at sixty-two and a half cents each.

Tr. 4. Dec. 12. Finished drawing twenty cords of Beech and Maple at one dollar and twenty-five cents a cord.

Tr. 5. Dec. 15. Bought four quires of Writing Paper at twenty cents each, and one Sons of Temperance Offering for two dollars and twenty-five cents.

Tr. 6. Dec. 20. Bought one North American Second Class Reader for fifty cents; one Ivory Folder for nineteen cents; and one Box of Wafers for six cents. Settled, and received the balance due in cash. How much was it?   *'Ans.* $21.30.

EXAMPLE VII.

The seventh example exhibits a Pork Account, and the eighth a Beef Account. The entries are to be made according to the principles stated under the fourth example, and more fully elucidated under the account with a Wheatfield, given at the 28th and 29th pages.

Transaction 1. Sept. 10, 1850. Bought forty-five Hogs weighing 9856 lbs. at three cents a pound.

What do the seventh and eighth examples exhibit? In these and similar accounts, how are we to determine what transactions to enter on the Dr. and what on the Cr. side of the account?

Tr. 2. Sept. 15. Bought seventeen Hogs weighing 4180 lbs. at two and three-fourth cents a pound, and 900 bushels of Corn at forty cents a bushel.

Tr. 3. Oct. 25. Paid for moving and grinding 280 bushels of Corn at six cents a bushel.

Tr. 4. Dec. 10. Expense of slaughtering sixty-two Hogs estimated at seventy-five cents each.

Tr. 5. Dec. 11. Laid by for family use 750 lbs. of Pork worth five cents a pound.

Tr. 6. Dec. 12. Expense of marketing 62 Hogs estimated at 20 cents each. Sold 18,650 lbs. of Pork for five cents a pound. What was the profit on fattening sixty-two Hogs?

Ans. $123.67.

EXAMPLE VIII.

This example exhibits a Beef Account.

Transaction 1. July 20, 1850. Bought twenty yoke of Oxen at sixty dollars a yoke.

Tr. 2. Aug. 4. Bought 15 Cows at twelve dollars a head.

Tr. 3. Aug. 10. Bought 22 Cows at $12.50 a head.

Tr. 4. Aug. 20. Bought twenty-three Steers at twenty dollars a head.

Tr. 5. Nov. 1. The pasturing up to this time is estimated at eleven weeks for all of the cattle, (some have been kept longer and others not so long,) and at twelve cents a week per head. They have been fed one hundred loads of pumpkins worth 50 cents a load.

Tr. 6. Feb. 1, 1851. Have fed one hundred tons of hay worth four dollars and fifty cents a ton; also 1800 bushels of corn worth thirty-five cents, and have paid for grinding the same five cents a bushel. Have this day sold the whole, at the following prices: Twenty yoke of Oxen, each Ox weighing 880 lbs., at five cents a pound; thirty-seven Cows at an average weight of 600 lbs. for four and one half cents a pound; and twenty-three Steers weighing 700 lbs. each, at five cents a pound. What have been the profits on fattening Beef?

Ans. $97.00.

EXAMPLE IX.

This example consists of a series of transactions with F. M. Granger, a saddle and harness maker.

Transaction 1. Jan. 4, 1850. Bought of him one common one-half tug Harness for sixteen dollars; three common Halters at 75 cents each; and two common Bridles at 75 cents each.

Tr. 2. Jan. 10. Sold him ten cords of Wood for one dollar and twenty-five cents a cord, and eighteen bushels of Potatoes at thirty cents a bushel.

Tr. 3. Jan. 25. Sold him 20 lbs. of table Butter at fourteen cents a pound.

Tr. 4. Feb. 10. Sold him eighteen bushels of Wheat at eighty-eight cents a bushel.

Tr. 5. Feb. 26. Sold him 25 lbs. table Butter at fifteen cents a pound.

Tr. 6. March 4. Sold him 2 tons of Hay at $4.50 a ton.

Tr. 7. March 22. Sold 10 bush. of Potatoes at thirty-five cents a bushel.

Tr. 8. April 10. Bought of him one common Saddle worth $7.00; one quilted Saddle at $25.00; and one pair of Martingales at seventy-five cents.

Tr. 9. June 6. Bought one Buggy Harness, black trimmings, at $20.00; one common single Harness, for $13.00; and two bridle Halters at $1.20 each.

Tr. 10. June 10. Sold him 10 bushels of Wheat at 90 cents a bushel.

Tr. 11. July 2. Bought one Plated Buggy Harness for $25.00, and one light Double Harness with Turrets and Hooks, for $30.00. Have done for him four days' work with team, worth $2.00 a day.

Tr. 12. July 24. Have pastured two Cows for him 12 weeks, at 20 cents per week for each Cow.

Tr. 13. Nov. 15. Have had Collars repaired for thirty-eight cents, and bought a Throat-latch for twenty cents.

Tr. 14. Nov. 25. Sold him 10 bushels of Wheat at 88 cents a bushel; 80 lbs. of Butter at 14 cents a pound; and 75 lbs. of Cheese at 7 cents a pound. Bought of him one Hard Leather Trunk for twenty dollars.

Tr. 15. Dec. 1. Sold him 4 tons of Hay for five dollars a ton.

Tr. 16. Dec. 20. He has trimmed my Buggy for which I am to pay him 18 dollars, and repaired a Buggy Harness for 2 dollars and 25 cents. I have bought of him one Long Tug Harness for 24 dollars, and one Bridle Halter for one dollar and twenty cents.

Tr. 17. Dec. 30. Have this day settled with him and paid him 29 dollars and 9 cents in cash, and given him my note to balance, at thirty days. What was the face of the note?

Ans. $60.00.

EXAMPLE X.

This example relates to a Field of Oats of Five Acres. The account should be kept in all respects like that with a Wheat-field, given at the 28th and 29th pages.

Transaction 1. April 20, 1850. Have spent 5 days in plowing five acres for oats, labor worth two dollars a day.

Tr. 2. April 26. Have furnished 18 bushels of oats for seed, worth 31 cents a bushel; and have devoted three-fourths of the day to sowing the same, labor worth one dollar a day.

Tr. 3. Apr. 27. Boy and team have been occupied two days in harrowing in oats, at one dollar and fifty cents a day.

Tr. 4. July 20. Have devoted five days to harvesting,

To what does the tenth example relate? How should the account be kept?

63

which (including the use of team) is worth one dollar and twenty-five cents a day.

Tr. 5. Sept. 22. Finished threshing 200 bushels of oats, the entire amount raised from the field. Threshing costs six cents a bushel.

Tr. 6. Oct. 26. Have devoted three days ͺto marketing 200 bushels of oats, which, including the use of team, is worth three cents a bushel. The crop has been raised on land worth 20 dollars an acre, and has required the use of it one year, money being worth 7 per cent. per annum. Received for the oats this day sold, 25 cents a bushel; retained straw for fodder, worth 5 dollars; and received 3 dollars for straw sold to the upholsterer. What are the profits on the field of oats of 5 acres?

Ans. $7.42.

EXAMPLE XI.

This example exhibits an account with a Wheatfield of Sixty Acres. The value of land and the rate of interest are the same as stated in the sixth transaction of the last preceding example.

Transaction 1. June 25. Finished plowing the field of sixty acres, which was worth one dollar and 75 cents an acre.

Tr. 2. July 20. Finished harrowing the field, which was worth thirty-three and one-third cents an acre.

Tr. 3. Sept. 10. Finished the cross-plowing, which was worth one dollar and 25 cents an acre.

Tr. 4. Sept. 15. Furnished 90 bushels of seed wheat, worth 75 cents a bushel; sowed the field, which was worth 10 cents an acre; and harrowed after the sowing, which was worth 75 cents an acre.

Tr. 5. July 10, 1851. This day finished cradling, binding, and shocking the sixty acres of wheat, which was worth one dollar an acre.

What account is exhibited in the eleventh example? What was the value of the land occupied, and what the rate of interest charged for its use?

Tr. 6. July 14. Finished drawing into the barn, which was worth thirty-three and one-third cents per acre.

Tr. 7. Aug. 1. Have paid 10 cents a bushel for threshing. The field yielded fifteen hundred bushels of wheat.

Tr. 8. Aug. 15. Marketed 1350 bushels, the time and trouble being worth 2 cents a bushel. The value of the land per acre, and the rate of interest as already stated. Kept for use on the farm, one hundred bushels of seed wheat, worth 75 cents a bushel; reserved for family use 50 bushels worth 75 cents a bushel; and sold, at the same price, 1350 bushels. Sold 20 dollars worth of straw to the paper-maker, and kept 10 dollars worth for fodder. What were the profits on the sixty acres of wheat?   *Ans.* $495.50.

EXAMPLE XII.

This example exhibits an account with a Potato-field of Twenty Acres, the land being worth thirty dollars an acre; interest at 7 per cent.

Transaction 1. May 1, 1850. The plowing of the twenty acres was worth one dollar and 50 cents an acre.

Tr. 2. May 10. Furnished 225 bushels of potatoes for seed, which were worth 30 cents a bushel. The planting cost one dollar and 50 cents an acre.

Tr. 3. June 25. Spent ten days with boy and horse in plowing out potatoes, which was worth one dollar and twenty-five cents a day; and paid for thirty days' work in hoeing, at seventy-five cents a day.

Tr. 4. Nov. 1. The digging required 70 days' labor, worth 75 cents a day; the marketing required 10 days with team, at 2 dollars a day; and the value of the land and the rate of interest as already stated. Sold 2450 bushels of potatoes for 25

What does the twelfth example exhibit? What was the value of the land, and what the rate of interest?

cents a bushel; used 200 bushels in fattening hogs, worth 15 cents a bushel; and reserved 600 bushels for home use, worth 25 cents a bushel. What were the profits on the crop?*

Ans. $515.50.

SECOND FORM OF ACCOUNTS

In every form of keeping accounts the *principle* is the same. The Second Form of Accounts differs from that already given in but few particulars. In the *second form* there are *two sets of money columns on each page*, while in the *first form* there is but *one* set. In the second form the debits and credits are both kept on the same page, and entered in the order of their occurrence, the debits in the left-hand set of money columns, and the credits in the right-hand set.

On the next page is the account with Henry Van Allen, given from the 36th to the 39th pages, (which see,) here arranged according to the provisions of the Second Form of Accounts. This method requires less space for an account than where two pages are employed, and especially where there is a considerable inequality in the number of entries on the two sides of the account; but there is a greater liability to make mistakes in entering the amounts in the correct set of money columns.

* If the pupils of a school are desirous of solving a greater number of Examples, or the Teacher thinks they would be profitably employed in so doing, they may be prepared as follows: Let the Teacher, or any accurate pupil, carefully write out an account with debits and credits like those from the 22d page to the 39th, or like the "Key" to the preceding "Examples for Practice." By inspecting this account it will be easy to write out the transactions upon which it is based in the order they have occurred. These, properly numbered and dated, may be copied by each pupil of a class, and thus constitute a *New Example.* The account upon which the example is based will of course be a *Key* to the *Example.* Such examples may be prepared to any desirable extent.

How may additional "Examples for Practice" be prepared? Is the *principle* the same in every form of accounts? In what particulars does the *second form of accounts* differ from that already given? What are the advantages, and what the disadvantages of this method?

Henry Van Allen Dr. Cr.

1850								
Jan.	6	To 2¼ Yds. Broadcloth 4.00	9	00				
"	"	" 2½ " Cassimere 2.30	5	75				
"	"	" Trimmings for Clothes	4	25				
"	10	By 20 Bushels Wheat .75			15	00		
Feb.	4	To 40 lbs. Brown Sugar .08	3	20				
"	"	" 30½ Yds. Sheeting .10	3	05				
"	"	" 10 " De Laine .34	3	40				
"	"	" Trimmings		31				
Apr.	9	" 4 Yds. Irish Linen .56	2	24				
"	"	" 1½ " Linen Edging .20		30				
Mar.	10	" 2 Linen Hdkfs. .37½		75				
"	"	" 16 Yds. Wai'd Silk 1.25	20	00				
"	"	" 1 Pair Kid Buskins	1	25				
July	1	" 30 Yds. Sheeting .11	3	30				
"	"	" 14 lbs. Loaf Sugar .14	1	96				
Aug.	4	" 2 Palm Leaf Hats .31¼		63				
"	10	" 10 Yds. Brown Linen .35	3	50				
"	"	" 24 " L. Gingham .31	7	44				
Oct.	10	" 4 " Broadcloth 3.00	12	00				
"	"	" 1⅙ doz. Buttons .25		29				
"	"	" Trimmings as per Bill	12	25				
"	15	By 90 Bushels Wheat 87			78	30		
Dec.	29	" Cash to Balance			1	57		
			94	87	94	87		

By referring to the remarks made upon this account at the 38th and following pages, the learner will be prepared to answer the subjoined questions.

What should the books of the Creditor specify? What of the last Dr. entry in the account with H. Van Allen? May the Debtor give credit in his books as per bill received? In such cases what should be done with the bill? Why should the items sold be specified in the books of the Creditor, when they may be entered per bill in the books of the Debtor? What rule is given for making Dr. and Cr. entries?

BILLS OF ACCOUNT.

When accounts are kept by the Second Form, Bills of Account, which were treated of at the 42d page, may be made out in a corresponding manner. The account of George Graham with James Armitage, given at the 42d page, is again presented below, in a manner corresponding with the Second Form of Accounts.

George Graham,
In Acct. with James Armitage, Dr. Cr.

1850								
Jan.	10	To 3 Galls. Molasses	.50	1	50			
''	''	'' 2 Sets Cups and Saucers			50			
Feb.	4	'' 15 Yds. Calico	.15	2	25			
''	''	'' 2¼ '' Flannel	.20		50			
''	''	'' 3 Papers Pins	.10		30			
''	''	By 10 lbs. Butter	.14				1	40
May	10	To 4 '' Coffee	.13		52			
''	''	'' 12 '' Brown Sugar	.09	1	08			
''	''	By Cash					1	60
''	''	'' Balance Due					3	65
				6	65		6	65

Received Payment,

James Armitage,
June 2, 1850. *Per Bulkley.*

May Bills of Account be made out in accordance with the second method of keeping accounts? What account that has been heretofore given is here presented in accordance with this form of keeping accounts?

This example is the same as that given at the 42d page, but differently arranged. As here presented, it is receipted by James Armitage, the merchant, per Bulkley, his clerk, June 2d, 1850. As before presented it was not receipted.

In this form of making out a Bill of Account, or an Account Current, the transactions, like the entries in the Second Form of Accounts, are recorded *in the order of their occurrence*, the amounts in all cases being carried to the Dr. or Cr. columns, as circumstances require. In consequence of the greater liability to make mistakes in carrying the amounts to the correct set of money columns, as already intimated, the learner will do well to be doubly careful that his entries are correctly made, until the *habit of accuracy* is firmly established; and then he should not relax his efforts. With the practical book-keeper, *accuracy* is of the first importance; for the detection of a few mistakes in an account, or even of but one mistake, tends greatly to diminish the confidence that might otherwise be reposed in him. The learner, hence, cannot labor too assiduously in establishing a habit that will be of so great importance to him in all future life, whether engaged in business for himself or for others.

On the next page there are two examples for practice, which will sufficiently illustrate this mode of making out accounts. The examples here presented are the same as those given at the 43d page, with the transactions arranged in the order of their occurrence, to compare with the Second Form of Accounts. Here, as before, the price and the quantity are given, and the pupil is left to carry out the amount. He should be careful to carry each amount to the right set of money columns. If the amounts are correctly entered, the accounts will exactly balance.

As here presented, how is it receipted? In this form of making out accounts, how are the transactions recorded? To what columns are the amounts carried? In which set of money columns should the debits be entered, the right or the left? In which set should the credits be entered? Why should the learner be doubly careful in making these entries? How long should he thus be careful? Should he then relax his efforts? What is said of the importance of *accuracy*?

James Farmer,
In Acct. with Ira Merchant, Dr.   Cr.

1851						
Jan.	10	To 3½ Yds. Flannel	.50			
"	"	" 6 " Calico	.15			
"	"	" 7¾ " Shirting	.16			
"	"	By 9 Bushels Oats	.23			
May	4	To 1 Hoe, per son John			88	
"	"	By 4 Doz. Hens' Eggs	.09			
June	10	To 2 Scythes and Snaths		3	50	
"	16	By 8 Doz. Hens' Eggs	.08			
July	1	" Cash to Balance				5	20

Isaac Paywell,
In Acct. with Ira Merchant, Dr.   Cr.

1851						
Feb.	12	By 40 Bushels Oats	.27			
"	"	" 12 do. Corn	.44			
"	15	" 60 do. Wheat	.84			
Mar.	10	To 4 Yds. Broadcloth	4.50			
"	"	" 16 " Black Silk	1.00			
"	"	" Cash to Balance		32	48	

EXAMPLES FOR PRACTICE.

SECOND FORM OF ACCOUNTS.

As the remarks made under this head at the 54th page are applicable to the examples that follow, the pupil will do well to review them before proceeding further. The former examples were solved according to the First Form given for keeping accounts; these are to be solved according to the Second Form of Accounts.

EXAMPLE I.

This example consists of a series of transactions with James Davidson, who keeps a grocery and provision store.

Transaction 1. Jan. 2, 1851. Bought of him 18 lbs. Brown Sugar at 8 cents a pound; 15 lbs. of Rice at 7 cents a pound; and 12 lbs. of Loaf Sugar at 14 cents a pound.

Tr. 2. Feb. 10. Paid him four dollars in Cash. Also bought of him 10 lbs. of Codfish at 6 cents a pound, and 2 gallons of Molasses at 44 cents a gallon.

Tr. 3. March 4. Bought of him 12 lbs. of Butter at 15 cents a pound, and 10 lbs. of Cheese at 8 cents a pound.

Tr. 4. March 24. Bought 8 lbs. of Corn Starch at 11 cents a pound; 2 lbs. of Saleratus at 9 cents a pound; and 4 lbs. of Ginger at 10 cents a pound.

Tr. 5. April 12. Bought 4 bushels of Potatoes at 42 cents a bushel, and 6 dozen Eggs at 10 cents a dozen. Paid him on account four dollars in Cash.

Tr. 6. May 1. Bought of him one Ham, weighing 18 lbs.,

Why are examples for practice introduced into this work? [See page 54 for answers to these questions.] Of what does each example consist, and how should it be treated? How may you know whether the computations are correctly made, and the transactions rightly entered? Of what does the first example in the second form of accounts consist?

at 9 cents a pound, and 14 lbs. of Corn Meal at one cent a pound.

Tr. 7. June 10. Bought 12 lbs. of Rice at 6 cents a pound.

Tr. 8. July 2. Bought one-half bushel of Potatoes at 50 cents a bushel, and 10 lbs. of Mackerel at 9 cents a pound.

Tr. 9. Aug. 1. Settled and paid the balance due him in Cash. How much was it? *Ans.* $7.62.

EXAMPLE II.

This example consists of a series of transactions with Henry Ingalls, who keeps a boot and shoe and furnishing store.

Transaction 1. Jan 4, 1850. Have drawn him 8 cords of Hickory, for which he is to allow me one dollar and 50 cents a cord. Have also bought of him one pair of Kip Boots for 4 dollars; 3 pair of Children's Gaiters at 60 cents a pair; and 2 pair of Boys' Suspenders at 14 cents a pair.

Tr. 2. April 10. Bought three pair of Children's Gloves at fifteen cents a pair.

Tr. 3. April 14. Bought four Linen Handkerchiefs at sixty cents each, and two pair of Misses' Gaiters for one dollar and twenty-five cents each.

Tr. 4. May 6. Bought one Leghorn Hat for one dollar and fifty cents, and 2 Palm Leaf Hats for 30 cents each.

Tr. 5. May 20. Sold him 80 lbs. of Wool for 40 cents a pound, and settled the account, he paying the balance due in Cash. What was the amount paid by him to balance the account? *Ans.* $30.47.

EXAMPLE III.

This example consists of a series of transactions with John Adams, a hardware merchant.

Transaction 1. Jan. 10, 1851. Bought of him 2 Axes at one dollar and 25 çents each, and 3 Ax Helves at 20 cents each.

Tr. 2. April 4. Bought of him three Shanked Hoes at 65 cents each, and one Hoe with welded eye for 44 cents.

Tr. 3. June 10. Bought 3 Scythes at eighty-eight cents each, and 2 Scythe Snaths at seventy-five cents each.

Tr. 4. June 20. Bought a Log Chain weighing 20 lbs., at 10 cents a pound, and one Bush Scythe for one dollar.

Tr. 5. July 2. Bought one Grain Cradle for three dollars, and two Hay Rakes for fifteen cents each.

Tr. 6. Sept. 10. Settled and paid the amount due him in Cash. How much was it? *Ans.* $15.93.

EXAMPLE IV.

This example consists of a Tobacco Account for the period of twelve years. The person whose account is here presented uses three Cigars a day, that cost him three cents a piece, and pays for Tobacco in other forms, for smoking and chewing, four dollars and fifty-nine cents a year. This is a low estimate of the expenses of an habitual smoker and chewer of Tobacco; thousands of persons that support these habits pay on their account twice or thrice the amount here stated. What is the pecuniary expense sustained on their account in twelve years, allowing interest on the amount invested at 7 per cent. with annual settlements?

The transactions, which we will suppose commenced with the beginning of the year 1821, will be as follows:

Transaction 1. 1821. At the end of the year there should be entered on the Dr. side of the account the amount expended for Tobacco for one year.

Tr. 2. 1822. At the end of this year there should be

Of what does the fourth example consist? What amount of Cigars and Tobacco does the person whose account is here presented use? Is this a high estimate?

4   73

entered on the same side of the account, first the interest* on the amount expended for the *preceding* year, and then the amount expended for the last year.

Tr. 3. 1823. At the end of this year there should be entered, first the interest on the amount expended for the *two* preceding years, (the interest on the sum expended the first year being considered a part of said amount,) and then the amount expended for the last year.

Tr. 4. 1824. There should be entered, first the interest on the amount expended for the *three* preceding years, (the interests that have accrued being considered a part of said amount,) and then the amount expended for the last year.

Tr. 5. 1825. There should be entered, first the interest on the amount expended for *all the preceding years*, (the interests that have accrued being considered a part of said amount,) and then the amount expended for the last year.

[These transactions sufficiently elucidate the principle upon which the remaining seven transactions should be entered, the last of which will be as follows :]

Tr. 12. 1832. There should be entered, first the interest on the amount expended for the *eleven* preceding years, (the interests that have accrued being considered a part of said amount,) and then the amount expended for the last year. Finally, the account should be closed by entering on the Cr. side the necessary amount to balance. What will be the expense of these two habits in twelve years, as deduced from these transactions?   *Ans.* $669.75.

EXAMPLE V.

This example consists of a continuation of the Tobacco Ac-

---

* In computing interest, if the mills and decimals amount to *more than half a cent*, count them as a cent; if they amount to *less than half a cent*, omit them entirely.

What is the expense incurred by an individual on account of smoking and chewing according to this estimate in twelve years?

count introduced in the last example. That account was for the period of twelve years. This example brings the account down eleven years further, making twenty-three years in all. It will require twelve transactions, of which the first two and the last are here given.

Transaction 1. 1832. There should be entered the amount expended for the first twelve years, as shown, by the preceding example. [The first entry is neither more nor less, practically, than the amount to balance the preceding account brought forward.]

Tr. 2. 1833. There should be entered, first the interest on the amount expended for the *twelve* preceding years, and then the amount expended for the last year.

Tr. 12. 1843. This transaction should be entered on the principle stated in the twelfth transaction of the last example. [The principle upon which the intervening transactions should be entered has been sufficiently elucidated.] What will be the expense of smoking and chewing, as stated in the fourth example, for the period of twenty-three years?

Ans. $2000.65.

EXAMPLE VI.

This example consists of a continuation of the Tobacco Account embraced in the two preceding examples. In those two examples taken together, the account is exhibited for twenty-three years; in this it is brought down eleven years further, making thirty-four years in all. It will require the same number of transactions as the last example. These will commence with the year 1843, and end with the year 1854.

What will be the expense of smoking and chewing, as stated in the fourth example, for the period of thirty-four years?

Ans. $4802.01.

What the expense in twenty-three years? What in thirty-four years?

EXAMPLE VII.

This example consists of the Cash Account of an individual who is employed at a salary of five hundred dollars a year. In the 11th and 19th transactions the articles purchased are not specified; but there is reference to a Memorandum-book in which they are supposed to be entered.

Transaction 1. Jan. 1, 1850. The individual debits himself with the amount of Cash on hand at the beginning of the year, which is twenty-five dollars and fifty cents.

Tr. 2. Jan. 29. Paid four weeks' board at 2 dollars a week.

Tr. 3. Feb. 27. Paid four weeks' board at 2 dollars a week.

Tr. 4. March 25. Paid four weeks' board at 2 dollars a week.

Tr. 5. ' April 1. Received one quarter's salary.

Tr. 6. April 10. Paid 30 dollars for a suit of clothes.

Tr. 7. April 24. Paid four weeks' board at 2 dollars a week. Also paid the same day 4 dollars for one silk hat.

Tr. 8. May 3. Paid a missionary subscription of 15 dollars.

Tr. 9. May 10. Paid ten dollars for the support of the ministry for the current year.

Tr. 10. May 23. Paid four weeks' board at 2 dollars a week.

Tr. 11. June 1. Paid for sundries, as per memorandum, four dollars and fifty-six cents.

Tr. 12. July 4. Paid anniversary expenses, amounting in all to four dollars and fifty-seven cents.

Tr. 13. July 22. Paid 8 weeks' board at 2 dollars a week.

Tr. 14. Aug. 15. Received one and one half quarter's salary.

Tr. 15. Aug. 25. Bought a dress and sundry small articles for sister, amounting in all to twelve dollars and fifty cents.

Tr. 16. Oct. 1. Received one half quarter's salary.

Tr. 17. Oct. 10. Paid 14 dollars for a cow for my mother.

Tr. 18. Oct. 22. Paid 13 weeks' board at 2 dollars a week.

Tr. 19. Nov. 10. Bought sundries as per memorandum, amounting to seven dollars and seventy-five cents.

Tr. 20. Dec. 31. Paid 11 weeks' board at 2 dollars a week. Received one quarter's salary. What amount of Cash on hand?

Ans. $319.12.

EXAMPLE VIII.

This example exhibits a Wine-bibber's Account for the period of twelve years. It embraces the amount paid for Wine, Cigars, etc., and occasionally a moderate expenditure for a social repast, including supper, cards, and sundry kindred disbursements. The expense is estimated at one dollar a day, which a reformed man (who has had twenty years' experience, during which time he squandered an immense patrimony) informs me is a very low estimate of the expenses attendant upon fashionable tippling. Interest is to be computed as in the Tobacco Account exhibited in the fourth example, and the transactions are to be entered according to the principles there stated. The Wine-bibber's Account may be supposed to commence with the year 1828. What will it amount to in twelve years ending with the year 1839? *Ans.* $6529.29.

EXAMPLE IX.

This example consists of a continuation of the Wine-bibber's Account introduced in the last example. That account was for the period of twelve years. This example brings the account down eleven years further, making twenty-three years in all. This example, like the fifth, will embrace twelve transactions. These commence with the year 1839, and include the year 1850. What will the Wine-bibber's Account amount to in twenty-three years? *Ans.* $19,504.22.

What does the eighth example exhibit? What does it embrace? What is the expense estimated at per day? Is this a high estimate for fashionable tippling? What will the account amount to in twelve years? What in twenty-three years?

EXAMPLE X.

This example consists of a continuation of the Wine-bibber's Account embraced in the two preceding examples. In those two examples taken together, the account is exhibited for twenty-three years; in this it is carried forward eleven years further, making thirty-four years in all. It will require the same number of transactions as the last example. These will commence with the year 1850 and end with the year 1861. What will the Wine-bibber's Account amount to in thirty-four years?   *Ans.* $46,814.55.

EXAMPLE XI.

This example consists of a series of transactions with Otho H. Hudson, a hardware merchant.

Transaction 1. Jan. 3, 1851. Bought of him 2 Nail-hammers at 50 cents each; one Cast-steel do. at one dollar; 2 Handsaws at 2 dollars each; one large backed Saw for 2 dollars; and one small do. for one dollar and 25 cents.

Tr. 2. Feb. 1. Bought 2 Jack-planes and 2 Fore-planes at one dollar and 25 cents each, and 2 Long Jointers at one dollar and 50 cents each.

Tr. 3. Feb. 10. Bought one pr. of Match-planes, $1\frac{1}{4}$ in., for two dollars; 2 pr. do. do., $1\frac{1}{2}$ in., for 2 dollars and 25 cents a pair; and 2 Smoothing-planes for one dollar each. Paid 8 dollars on account.

Tr. 4. March 20. Bought one 7-foot Cross-cut Saw at 63 cents a foot, and one 7-foot Mill Saw at 94 cents a foot. Settled and paid the balance due in Cash. How much was it?   *Ans.* $28.74.

What will the account amount to in thirty-four years?

EXAMPLE XII.

This example is a continuation of the account with Otho H. Hudson.

Transaction 1. April 1, 1851. Bought 2 Bed-cords at 25 cents each; one Dinner-bell at one dollar; one Clothes-brush at 50 cents; one Nail do. at 31 cents; and 2 Tooth do. at 20 cents each.

Tr. 2. May 10. Bought one Strainer Milk-pail for 60 cents; 3 Milk-pans at 20 cents each; and 1 Wire Sieve for 44 cents. Settled and paid the amount due on the account. How much was it?   *Ans.* $4.35.

EXAMPLE XIII.

This example consists of a Sheep and Wool Account. I give it as furnished me by a worthy citizen who kept the Sheep. The transactions, although numerous, may be arranged under two dates.

Transaction 1. June, 1850. Have thirty Sheep, chiefly Lambs, valued at one dollar and 25 cents each.

Tr. 2. June, 1851. The Sheep were kept a portion of the year on a summer-fallow, where they were rather useful to the fallow than expensive, and the remainder of the year on the common. The pasturing and care may be considered worth 4 dollars and 80 cents for the year. They were not foddered at all; but during the winter they were fed half a bushel of oats a day for 60 days, oats being worth 25 cents a bushel. The expense of washing and shearing was 4 cents a head. The marketing was worth 50 cents. Had the sheep been sold a year ago, the money would have drawn 10 per cent. interest. Kept 7 lbs. of Wool, worth 40 cents a pound, for family use. Sold 103 lbs. for 40 cents a pound. The 30 old Sheep are

Of what does the 13th example consist? Is it a real example or a fictitious one? What were the profits on thirty Sheep for one year? How much is this a head?

worth 1 dollar and 50 cents each. Have raised 27 Lambs from them, worth one dollar and 25 cents each. What have been the profits on 30 Sheep for one year? *Ans.* $67.50.

EXAMPLE XIV.

This example is an account with O. D. Morgan, a grocer.
Transaction 1. Jan. 25, 1851. Bought of him $10\frac{1}{2}$ lbs. of Brown Sugar at 10 cents a pound; 12 lbs. of Butter at 14 cents; and 4 bushels of Potatoes at 40 cents a bushel.
Tr. 2. Feb. 20. Bought 8 lbs. of Rice at 6 cents a pound, and 12 lbs. of Corn Starch at $12\frac{1}{2}$ cents a pound.
Tr. 3. May 2. Bought 8 lbs. of Codfish at 6 cents a pound. Settled, and paid the amount due in Cash. How much money did he receive?* *Ans.* $6.79.

THIRD FORM OF ACCOUNTS

In the Third Form of Accounts there are two principal books— the Day-book and the Ledger. This form of accounts is sometimes called the Merchants' Form.

The DAY-BOOK is a book in which all the debit and credit transactions of the day are entered at the time and in the order of their occurrence, whether with one or many persons. It is ruled like the Ledger in the first form of accounts, with but one exception: in the Ledger there are *five* spaces, the two at the left being occupied for the month and the day of the month; while in the Day-book there are but *four* spaces. The date in the Day-book is kept in the middle of the page, and the left-hand space is used for entering the folio of the Ledger into which the entry is posted.

* For the mode of providing additional examples, see note on the 66th page.

How many principle books are used in the third form of accounts? What are they? What is this form sometimes called? What is the Day-book? How is it ruled? Where is the date kept? For what is the left-hand space used? How may additional examples for practice be prepared? [See the note.]

80

In the Third Form of Accounts, when several articles are sold to the same person at one time, (or bought of him, as the case may be,) it is best only to *short extend* the particular sums, or to enter them without the money columns, and then *full extend* the amount of the whole, entering the same within the money columns. By this means the number of entries necessary to be made in the Ledger will be considerably diminished, and the account can hence be exhibited in much less space than would be otherwise required. Before any such amount is full extended, it will be well, in order to avoid mistakes, for the book-keeper always carefully to review the entries, with a pen or pencil in hand, affixing to those that have been so examined a sign (thus √) to show that the work has been reviewed. When thus tested, the *amount* may be *full extended*. In this form of accounts, as the price per yard, pound, etc., and the partial amounts as short extended are both without the money columns, it is customary to use the counting-room *at* (@) in connection with the price.

The LEDGER is a book to which the entries recorded in the Day-book are transferred, and so arranged as to present the account with each person on a folio by itself. It is ruled as follows. The pages are divided by double perpendicular lines into two equal parts, each of which is ruled like the Ledger in the first form of accounts, with this exception: there is an additional space at the left of the money columns in which is entered the page of the Day-book from which the entry is posted. This done, place two parallel lines (thus //) opposite the account in the Day-book to show that it has been posted. The *amount only* of the articles purchased at any one time is

When should the items of an account be *short extended?* What advantage is derived from *full extending* the *amount only* of the articles bought or sold at one time? What is said in relation to reviewing the entries before the amount is full extended? What is said of the counting-room *at* (@) used in the third form of accounts? What is the Ledger? How is it ruled? What is the use of the additional space? What do the parallel lines placed opposite the account in the Day-book show? In posting, what only is carried to the Ledger?

carried to the Ledger. The debit entry, "To Day-book, 21, 1.69," which is the first in the following Ledger in the account with H. M. Roberts, is elliptical, (see p. 94.) Supply the ellipses and the entry will stand thus : "To the amount of the articles entered in the Day-book on the 21st page, $1.69." The same remark applies to all Ledger entries. Instructions are sometimes given to enter in the Ledger "To Merchandise" or "By Merchandise," "Sundries," "Groceries," "Goods," "Cash," "Note," "Order," etc., etc., as the case may chance to be. But as such entries give the Ledger an incongruous appearance, and are at best unsatisfactory; and as in case the account is questioned it becomes necessary in the settlement to refer to the original entries in the Day-book, it is thought the propriety of uniformly adopting the mode here recommended cannot fail to be apparent.

Moreover, to avoid the customary inconvenience in text-books of turning the book around in order to exhibit the Ledger accounts, which is both unnatural and awkward, and the scarcely less objectionable method of exhibiting the Dr. and Cr. entries on different pages, which is rarely if ever practiced in this form of accounts, it has been found necessary to diminish the third space in the Ledger, and to use the letter $\mathscr{D}$ instead of the whole word, Day-book. But in doing this, while we really sacrifice nothing, we gain much; for we exhibit to the learner the exact form in which accounts are usually kept. Indeed, many of our best accountants omit this space entirely. It will be seen, then, that the middle course has been adopted in this treatise.

POSTING BOOKS is transferring the accounts of various persons from the Day-book, through which they are scattered, to the Ledger, and arranging each on a folio by itself, with the

---

Is the entry, "To Day-book," elliptical? How will it stand with the ellipses supplied? Is the same true of all Ledger entries? What does the letter $\mathscr{D}$ in the third space in the Ledger stand for? Why has this abridgment been made? What is sacrificed, and what gained by it? What is Posting Books?

proper reference figures in the Day-book to show the folio of the Ledger *into* which each entry is posted, and with corresponding reference figures in the Ledger to show the page of the Day-book *from* which each entry is posted. This is done as follows: Take the Day-book and turn to the first unposted entry, and by means of the Index find the Ledger account to which it belongs, if such an account has been opened. If no such account has been opened in the Ledger, write the proper title in the Index, opposite which place the folio of the Ledger that is to be devoted to the account, and then, having entered its title, proceed with the posting. Entries may be posted from the Cashbook directly into the Ledger, the same as from the Day-book.

If at any time it is ascertained that a transaction has not been recorded in its proper place, and under its appropriate date, the entry should be immediately made, with the proper explanation. In the First and Second Forms of Account, the first entry of an account will of course be made in the Ledger, as that is the only book used; but in the Third Form of Accounts the original entry should in all cases be made in the Day-book, from which it must be posted into the Ledger.

Should an entry at any time, by accident or carelessness, be made in the wrong side of an account, it should not be erased; but the same amount should be entered on the opposite side of the account, " To Error," or " By Error," as the case may be. It is apparent that the only effect of this last entry will be to *counteract the mistake ;* this done, the correct entry should be made. In case a transaction is entered to the wrong account, the correction is made in a similar manner ; but too great pains

---

How is this done? If at any time it is ascertained that a transaction has not been recorded in its proper place, and under its appropriate date, what should be done? Where is the first entry of an account made in the first and second forms of account? Where in the third form of accounts? In case a transaction is entered on the wrong side of an account, should the entry be erased? What should be done? What will be the effect of this entry? Should the correct entry then be made? In case a transaction is entered to the wrong account, how is the correction made? Can too great pains be taken to make the original entries correct?

cannot be taken to make the original entries correct. It should be the aim and pride of the book-keeper *never to make a mistake in the entry of his accounts.*

It has been already remarked, (page 19th,) that when a person has several Ledgers, they should be designated by the letters of the alphabet, thus: Ledger A; Ledger B; etc. Day-books should be lettered in the same manner; and the first entry that is posted from a new Day-book into the Ledger should show in the Ledger the Day-book from which it is posted. For example, if you commence Day-book A, and Ledger A, at the same time, the Day-book may be filled when the Ledger is not more than one-fourth full. In this case the first entry that is posted from Day-book B into Ledger A should be entered thus: *To or By* (as the case may be) *Day-book* B, *p. 1.*

When one Ledger is filled and a new one is opened, any unsettled accounts may be carried to the new Ledger in the same manner that an account is carried from one folio to another, for which see the account with H. Van Allen in the First Form of Accounts. The following account commences with the 21st page of the Day-book, and the 33d page of the Ledger. We will call the former, Day-book F; and as we have already used three Ledgers, we will call the latter, Ledger D. It will be seen that the accounts with different persons in the following Day-book, and the Dr. and Cr. entries to the same account, where they occur, are separated by a horizontal line. To render the accounts more distinct, as well as to improve the appearance of the page, it is customary to use *red ink* in drawing these lines.

What should be the aim and pride of the book-keeper? When several Day-books and Ledgers are used by the same person, how are they designated? When you commence to post from a new Day-book, what should the first entry show? Give an example. When one Ledger is filled and a new one opened, what should be done with unsettled accounts? At what pages, and with what books, does the following account commence? How are different accounts separated in the Day-book?

	H. M. Roberts	Dr.		
	To 1 Pr. Steelyards	.63		
33	" 1 Gimlet	.06		
	" 2 Sickles @ 50 c.	1.00	1	69
	Isaac Hinman	Dr.		
	To 2 Curtain Pins @ 35 c.	.70		
33	" 1 Mincing Knife	.40		
	" 1 Razor Strop	.40	1	50
	Job Peabody	Dr.		
	To 1 Currycomb	.25		
33	" 2 Horse Cards @ 10 c.	.20		
	" 1 do. Brush	.75	1	20

——————— Thursday, July 3d. ———————

	Bronson Fisher	Dr.		
	To 1 Tin Lantern	.38		
35	" 1 Dinner Horn	.19		
	" 6 Candle Moulds @ 6 c.	.36		
	" 1 Dusting Pan	.25	1	18
	N. O. Morehouse	Dr.		
	To 1 Grain Scoop Shovel	1.00		
34	" 4 lbs. Rope @ 15 c.	.60		
	" 8 " Cotton Rope @ 25 c.	2.00	3	60
	James Ellis	Dr.		
	To 1 Pocket Compass	.50		
34	" 2 Pr. Snuffers @ 37½ c.	.75		
	" 1 Pocket Knife	1.00	2	25

	A. F. Kingsley	Dr.		
	To 1 Pr. Spring Dividers	.63		
34	" 1 Pocket Compass	.50		
	" 2 Trunk Locks @ 31 c.	.62		
	" 1 Chest do.	.44	2	19
	Silas Boomer	Dr.		
	To 1 Dead Lock	.50		
35	" 2 Cottage do. @ 1.50	3.00		
	" 3 Trunk do. @ 35 c.	1.05	4	55

Monday, July 7th.

	James Ellis	Dr.		
	To 1 Framing Chisel, ½ in.	.50		
	" 2 do. do. ¾ " @ 75 c.	1.50		
34	" 1 do. do. 1½ "	.88		
	" 1 Crow=bar, 10 lbs. @ 10 c.	1.00		
	" 1 Cow Bell	.75	4	63
	N. O. Morehouse	Dr.		
	To 1 Hand Saw File	.10		
34	" 1 Set Knives and Forks	1.25		
	" 1 Screw=driver	.38		
	" 12 lbs. Lead Pipe @ 8 c.	96	2	69

Saturday, July 12th.

35	Bronson Fisher	Cr.		
	By 15 lbs. Butter @ 10 c.		1	50
	Job Peabody	Cr.		
33	By 18 lbs. Cheese @ 8 c.	1.44		
	" 1 Ton Hay	4.50	5	94

	Isaac Hinman	Dr.		
	To 1 Sprinkling Pot	.38		
33	" 1 Buck Saw	1.00		
	" 1 Box 8 × 10 Glass	2.25	3	63
	H. M. Roberts	Dr.		
33	To 4 lbs. Putty @ 8 c.	.32		
	" 12 " Russia Pipe @ 20 c.	2.40	2	72
	Silas Boomer	Cr.		
35	By 4 Days' Labor on House @ 1.50		6	00
	Dr.			
	To 10 lbs. Cast Steel @ 22 c.	2.20		
35	" 14 " German do. @ 15 c.	2.10	4	30
	James Ellis	Dr.		
34	To 1 Porcelain Kettle	1.25		
	" 1 Gross 1 in. Screws	.44	1	69
	Thursday, July 17th.			
	Job Peabody	Dr.		
	To 1 Box 7 × 9 Glass	2.10		
33	" 1 " 8 × 10 do.	2.25		
	" 3 Pocket Knives @ 53 c.	1.59	5	9
	Bronson Fisher	Dr.		
35	To 1 Set Knives and Forks	1.25		
	" 1 Quart Measure	.25	1	50
	Cr.			
35	By 4 Bushels Potatoes @ 25 c.	1.00		
	" 2 do. Wheat @ 75 c.	1.50	2	50

	A. F. Kingsley	Dr.		
	To 1 Hand Vice	1.50		
34	" 1 Screw=driver	.40		
	" 2 Spittoons @ 30 c.	.60		
	" 2 Hand Saw Files @ 10 c.	.20	2	70
	———— Cr. ————			
	By 2 Bushels Potatoes @ 30 c.	.60		
34	" 30 lbs. Cheese @ ?c.	2.40		
	" 10 " Butter @ 12 c.	1.20	4	20
	———— Wednesday, July 23d. ————			
	James Ellis	Cr.		
34	By 14 lbs. Wool @ 40 c.	5.60		
	" Note against H. Allen	1.50	7	10
	———— Dr. ————			
34	To 42 lbs. Lead Pipe @ 8 c.	3.36		
	" 20 " Com. Stove Pipe @ 10 c.	2.00	5	36
	———— " ————			
	H. M. Roberts	Dr.		
	To 1 Single Barrel Shot Gun	8.00		
33	" 1 Double " "	16.00		
	" 2 Powder Flasks @ 1.00	2.00	26	00
	———— Cr. ————			
33	By Cash on Account		30	00
	———— Friday, July 25th. ————			
	Bronson Fisher	Dr.		
	To 2 Stand Lamps @ 25 c.	.50		
	" 1 Mouse Trap	.25		
35	" 1 Grain Scoop Shovel	1.00		
	" 2 Wheel Heads @ 25 c.	.50		
	" 1 Pocket Compass	.50	2	75

	Isaac Hinman	Dr.		
	To 2 Sets Knitting Pins @ 4 c.	.08		
33	" 1 Pr. Spring Dividers	.63		
	" 1 " Snuffers	.37		
	" 2 Wheel Heads @ 50 c.	1.00	2	08
	Cr.			
33	By Note against Peter Hyde	8.40		
	" Cash on Account	2.50	10	90

Thursday, July 31st.

	A. F. Kingsley	Cr.		
34	By 10 Bushels Corn @ 40 c.	4.00		
	" 26 do. Oats @ 20 c.	5.20	9	20

	Silas Boomer	Dr.		
	To 2 Lath Hatchets @ 75 c.	1.50		
35	" 1 Iron Mortar	1.25		
	" 1 Dusting Pan	.50		
	" 1 Strainer Milk-pail	.63	3	88

	Job Peabody	Cr.		
	By Pasturing Cow 10 Weeks @ 25 c.	2.50		
33	" do. Horse 6 do. @ 30 c.	1.80		
	" 2 Tons Hay @ 4.50	9.00	13	30

	James Ellis	Cr.		
	By 10 lbs. Butter @ 10 c.	1.00		
	" 8 Doz. Eggs @ 7 c.	.56		
34	" 10 Bushels Oats @ 20 c.	2.00		
	" 2 do. Potatoes @ 25 c.	.50		
	" 1 do. Turnips	.20	4	26

	Job Peabody	Dr.		
	To 3 Bed Cords @ 25 c.	.75		
	'' 1 Set Iron Table Spoons	.25		
	'' 1 Wire Sieve	.44		
33	'' 1 Tin Lantern	.38		
	'' 1 Dinner Horn	.19		
	'' 1 Razor Strop	.37		
	'' 1 Try Square	1.00	3	38
	N. O. Morehouse	Dr.		
	To 1 Coffee Mill	.88		
	'' 1 Razor Hone	.37		
34	'' 1 Pr. Snuffers	.38		
	'' 2 Wheel Heads @ 50 c.	1.00		
	'' 1 Pr. Brass Candlesticks	.75		
	'' 2 Stand Lamps @ 25 c.	.50	3	88
	Cr.			
34	By Cash on Account		5	00
	Monday, Aug. 4th.			
	A. F. Kingsley	Dr.		
	To 1 Britannia Tea Pot	.88		
	'' 12 lbs. Cotton Rope @ 25 c.	3.00		
34	'' 1 Wooden Faucet	.13		
	'' 1 Mouse Trap	.25		
	'' 2 Trunk Locks @ 31 c.	.62	4	88
	Bronson Fisher	Dr.		
	To 1 Pr. Buggy Springs, 40 lbs.@11c.	4.40		
35	'' 1 do. Tongs	.50		
	'' 2 Barn Shovels @ 87½ c.	1.75	6	65

	H. M. Roberts	*Dr.*	
	To 1 Tin Dipper	.19	
	" 1 do. Grater	.12	
	" 1 Gallon Measure	.50	
33	" 1 Sprinkling Pot	.38	
	" 2 Skimmers @ 10 c.	.20	
	" 1 Bucksaw	1.00	
	" 2 Spittoons @ 37½ c.	.75	3 14
	Cr.		
33	By Cash on Account		1 00
	Isaac Hinman	*Dr.*	
	To 1½ lbs. Butter @ 8 c.	1.12	
33	" 20 " Cheese @ 7 c.	1.40	
	" 4 Bushels Potatoes @ 25 c.	1.00	
	" 2 do. Turnips @ 20 c.	.40	3 92
	Monday, Aug. 11th.		
	Job Peabody	*Cr.*	
	By 40 Bushels Corn @ 40 c.	16.00	
33	" 40 do. Oats @ 25 c.	10.00	
	" 12 lbs. Butter @ 8 c.	.96	26 90
	Bronson Fisher	*Cr.*	
35	By Note against Job Brown		3 75
	N. O. Morehouse	*Dr.*	
	To 1 Spice Mill	.75	
34	" 2 Pr. Snuffers @ 35 c.	.70	
	" 2 Sets Knitting Pins @ 4 c.	.08	
	" 1 Pocket Compass	.50	2 03

	H. M. Roberts	Cr.		
33	By Cash to Balance Account		2	55
	———— // ————			
	Isaac Hinman	Cr.		
33	By 2 lbs. Butter @ 10 c.	.20		
	" Cash to Balance Account	.03		23
	———— Wednesday, Aug. 13th. ————			
	Job Peabody	Dr.		
33	To My Note on Demand		35	68
	———— // ————			
	Bronson Fisher	Cr.		
35	By Cash to Balance Account		4	33
	———— // ————			
	N. O. Morehouse	Cr.		
34	By Cash to Balance Account		7	20
	———— // ————			
	James Ellis	Cr.		
34	By 10 Bushels Oats @ 20 c.	2.00		
	" Cash to Balance Account	.57	2	57
	———— // ————			
	A. F. Kingsley	Dr.		
34	To 1 Double Barrel Shot Gun		16	00
	———— Cr. ————			
34	By Cash to Balance Account		12	37
	———— // ————			
	Silas Boomer	Dr.		
35	To 1 Pr. Buggy Springs, 40 lbs.@11c.	4.40		
	" 1 Currycomb	.25	4	65
	———— Cr. ————			
35	By Note to Balance Account		11	38

A		M	
		Morehouse, N. O.	34
B C D		**N O**	
Boomer, Silas	35		
E		**P**	
Ellis, James	34	Peabody, Job	33
F G		**Q**	
Fisher, Bronson	35		
H		**R**	
Hinman, Isaac	33	Roberts, H. M.	33
I J		**S T U V**	
K L		**W X Y Z**	
Kingsley, A. F.	34		

Dr.   H. M. Roberts   Cr.

1851						1851					
July	1	To D.	21	1	69	July	23	By D.	24	30	00
"	14	"	23	2	72	Aug.	7	"	27	1	00
"	23	"	24	26	00	"	12	"	28	2	55
Aug.	7	"	27	3	14						
				33	55					33	55

Dr.   Isaac Hinman   Cr.

1851						1851					
July	1	To D.	21	1	50	July	28	By D.	25	10	90
"	14	"	23	3	63	Aug.	12	"	28		23
"	28	"	25	2	08						
Aug.	7	"	27	3	92						
				11	13					11	13

Dr.   Job Peabody   Cr.

1851						1851					
July	1	To D.	21	1	20	July	12	By D.	22	5	94
"	17	"	23	5	94	"	31	"	2	13	30
Aug.	2	"	26	3	38	Aug.	11	"	27	26	96
"	13	"	28	35	68						
				46	20					46	20

Dr. N. O. Morehouse Cr. 34

1851						1851					
July	3	To D.	21	3	60	Aug.	2	By D.	26	5	00
"	7	"	22	2	69	"	13	"	28	7	20
Aug.	2	"	26	3	88						
"	11	"	27	2	03						
				12	20					12	20

Dr. James Ellis Cr.

1851						1851					
July	3	To D.	21	2	25	July	23	By D.	24	7	10
"	7	"	22	4	63	"	31	"	25	4	26
"	14	"	23	1	69	Aug.	13	"	28	2	57
"	23	"	24	5	36						
				13	93					13	93

Dr. A. F. Kingsley Cr.

1851						1851					
July	5	To D.	22	2	19	July	21	By D.	24	4	20
"	21	"	24	2	70	"	31	"	25	9	20
Aug.	4	"	26	4	88	Aug.	13	"	28	12	37
"	13	"	28	16	00						
				25	77					25	77

Dr.   Bronson Fisher   Cr.

1851						1851					
July	3	To D.	21	1	18	July	12	By D.	22	1	50
"	17	"	23	1	50	"	17	"	23	2	50
"	25	"	24	2	75	Aug.	11	"	27	3	75
Aug.	4	"	26	6	65	"	13	"	28	4	33
				12	08					12	08

Dr.   Silas Boomer   Cr.

1851						1851					
July	5	To D.	22	4	55	July	14	By D.	23	6	00
"	14	"	23	4	30	Aug.	13	"	28	11	38
"	31	"	25	3	88						
Aug.	13	"	28	4	65						
				17	38					17	38

EXAMPLES FOR PRACTICE.

THIRD FORM OF ACCOUNTS.

In the First and Second Forms of Account each example consists of several transactions with the same individual. See pp. 54th and 66th. But in the Third Form of Accounts the transactions of the day are intermingled, being entered in the Day-book at the time and in the order of their occurrence.

The following examples consist of a series of transactions with twenty-five persons. These should be entered in the Day-book prepared to accompany this volume, after the manner of those already given in this Form, commencing at the 85th page. This done, they should be posted into the Ledger as those were, according to the instructions given at the 82d page. These transactions, which commence with the month of June, 1851, continue three months. But after the first month, with a very few exceptions, there is a settlement of at least one account every day. For the convenience of teachers in examining the work of their pupils, these examples are entered in the Day-book and posted into the Ledger, in the Key; but the learner should consult this for the purpose of instruction as rarely as may be.

Monday, June 2d, 1851.

Transaction 1. Sold Ira Allen 2 pr. of buskins, at $1.25 a pr.; 1 pr. of gloves, for 56 c.; $1\frac{3}{4}$ yds. linen edging, at 20 c. a yd.; and 4 whalebones, at 3 c. each.

Tr. 2. Sold Reu Corbett 2 yds. of colored cambric, at 11 c.; 5 yds. linen drill, at 41 c.; $2\frac{1}{2}$ yds. check cambric, at

In the First and Second Forms of Account, of what does each example consist? In the Third Form of Accounts, how are the transactions of the day recorded? Of what do the examples for practice in this form of accounts consist? What instructions are given for entering these transactions in the Day-book and Ledger? With what month do these transactions commence, and how long do they continue? When do the settlements take place? For what purpose are these examples solved in the Key?

50 c.; 1 pr. white cotton hŏse, at 50 c.; and three pr. white cot. hose, at 25 c.

Tr. 3. Received of William Loomis 45 lbs. of wool, at 40 c., and 10 lbs. of butter, at 11 c. Sold him 8 yds. of calico, at 28 c.; 6 yds. of bleached muslin, at 25 c.; 1 card of shirt buttons, at 22 c.; one vest pattern, at 88 c.; and 1½ yds. Irish linen, at $1.00.

Tr. 4. Sold John Benson 4½ yds. of gingham, at 30 c., and one parasol, at $1.50.

Tuesday, June 3d, 1851.

Sold Job Estabrook 16 yds. bl'k silk, at $1.10 a yard; 3 yds. of muslin, at 11 c.; 4 skeins of silk, at 5 c.; and 2 lbs. of black tea, at 75 c.

Wednesday, June 4th, 1851.

Tr. 1. Sold Samuel H. Morris 2 bbls. of salt, at $1.25; 3 yds. of linen check, at 50 c.; and 1 pr. suspenders, at 37 c. Received of him 18 lbs. of wool, at 40 c.; and 2 doz. eggs, at 8 c.

Tr. 2. Sold John W. Thomson one piece of balzarine containing 11¾ yds., at 76 c.; one parasol, at $1.75; and one pr. of morocco shoes, at $1.50.

Thursday, June 5th, 1851.

Sold Ira Allen 1¾ yds. linen drill, at 44 c.; 1¾ yds. of cottonade, at 25 c.; 1¼ yds. of linen, at 25 c.; 2 pr. of kid buskins, at $1.25; 1 pr. of gloves, at 75 c.; and 1 yd. of white flannel, at 56 c.

Friday, June 6th, 1851.

Sold Reu Corbett 1 pr. of kid buskins, at $1.25; 1 pr. of child's shoes, at 63 c.; 1 pr. leather slips, at 75 c.; 3 yds. black cambric, at 11 c.; 2 linen handkerchiefs, at 35 c.; and 2 other linen hdkfs., at 50 c. Received of him 18 lbs. of wool, at 40 c., and 10 bush. of oats, at 25 c.

Saturday, June 7th, 1851.

Sold William Loomis 2 lbs. of Java coffee, at 13 c.; 2 lbs. of black tea, at 70 c.; 2 lbs. of ginger, at 15 c.; 3 lbs. corn starch, at 12 c.; 1 clothes brush, at 38 c.; and 2 gallons of molasses, at 56 c.

Monday, June 9th, 1851.

Sold Henry R. Thomas 8 lbs. of brown sugar, at 10 c.; 4 oz. of indigo, at 10 c.; 1 back-comb, at 25 c.; 2 lbs. of candles, at 14 c.; 2 pr. of suspenders, at 25 c.; and 2 pr. of cotton hose, at 30 c.

Tuesday, June 10th, 1851.

Tr. 1. Received of John Benson 40 lbs. of wool, at 35 c., and 4 lbs. of butter, at 10 c. Sold him 4 yds. of white cambric, at 25 c.; 3 yds. of bleached drill, at 12 c.; and 2 silk hdkfs., at 50 c.

Tr. 2. Sold Job Estabrook 1 pr. of bl'k worsted hose, at 56 c.; 1 pr. gambroon buskins, at $1.25; 1 Tuscan bonnet, at $4.00; 1 card of hooks and eyes, at 8 c.; and 6 whalebones, at 3 c.

Thursday, June 12th, 1851.

Sold Samuel H. Morris 30½ yds. of brown sheeting, at 10 c.; 7 yds. of alpacca, at 80 c.; 1 Jenny Lind braid bonnet, at $2.00; 3 yds. of gimp cord, at 4 c.; and 2 papers of needles, at 10 c.

Friday, June 13th, 1851.

Sold John W. Thomson 2¼ yds. of gambroon, at 44 c.; 1 bunch of linen thread, at 20 c.; and 2 skeins of silk, at 5 c.

Monday, June 16th, 1851.

Sold George H. Brewster 2 yds. of gingham, at 31 c.; 4 yds. of ribbon, at 4 c.; 3 pr. of cotton hose, at 50 c.; 1 pr. of kid buskins, at $1.50; and 1 pr. of ½ hose, at 28 c.

Tuesday, June 17th, 1851.

Sold William Eldred 5 yds. of brown linen, at 31 c.; 7 yds. of checked linen, at 50 c.; ⅔ doz. buttons, at 6 c.; 2 spools of thread, at 3 c.; and paid his order for $7.28.

Wednesday, June 18th, 1851.

Paid Lyman Marsh's order for $4.00; sold him 5 lbs. of Java coffee, at 15 c.; 10 lbs. sugar, at 10 c.; 1 lb. of pepper, at 19 c; 4 lbs. corn starch, at 12 c.; and 2 lbs. of saleratus, at 8 c.

Thursday, June 19th, 1851.

Sold Ira Allen 1 ladies' cravat, for 25 c.; 31 yds. of shirting, at 10 c.; and 2 doz. shirt buttons, at 6 c.

Friday, June 20th, 1851.

Sold Reu Corbett 3 galls. of molasses, at 56 c.; 1 tweed coat, for $10.00; 4 lbs. crushed sugar, at 13 c.; and 2 galls. of lamp-oil, at 88 c.

Saturday, June 21st, 1851.

Tr. 1.   Sold William Loomis 2 scythe-stones, at 10 c.; 1¼ yds. of satin jean, at 16 c.; 6 yds. of blea. muslin, at 9 c.; 2 spools of thread, at 6 c.; and 2 pr. of silk gloves, at 50 c.

Tr. 2.   Sold Henry R. Thomas 1 umbrella, for $1.63; 1 parasol, for $1.75; 14 lbs. crushed sugar, at 12½ c.; 1 shoe-brush, for 25 c.; and 1 box of blacking, for 10 c.

Monday, June 23d, 1851.

Received of Job Estabrook 57½ lbs. of wool, at 30 c. a lb.

Sold him one land side for plow, for $1.00 ; 2 scythe-stones, at 10 c.; and 2 quires of letter-paper, at 25 c.

Tuesday, June 24th, 1851.

Tr. 1. Received of Ira Allen 14 lbs. of wool, at 40 c., and five dollars in cash. Sold him 7 yds. of blue calico, at 16 c.; 6 yds. of Franklin drill, at 25 c.; and 1 De Laine shawl, for $3.75.

Tr. 2. Received of Reu Corbett 10 lbs. of butter, at 8 c.; 5½ doz. eggs, at 8 c.; and one dollar in cash.

Wednesday, June 25th, 1851.

Tr. 1. Received of William Loomis 7 doz. eggs, at 8 c., and 23½ lbs. of butter, at 10 c.

Tr. 2. Sold Henry R. Thomas 1 remnant of edging for 25 c.; ½ lb. of cotton yarn, at 31 c.; 1 gallon of molasses, for 50 c.; 3 yds. of pink ribbon, at 6 c.; $7\frac{3}{16}$ lbs. of codfish, at 6 c.; and 2 papers of needles, at 9 c. Received of him $4.00 in cash.

Tr. 3. Sold John Benson 6 lbs. of sugar, at 10 c.; 2 lbs. of black tea, at 75 c.; 2 lbs. of pepper, at 19 c.; 4 whalebones, at 4 c.; and 4 pr. of cotton ½ hose, at 25 c.

Thursday, June 26th, 1851.

Tr. 1. Sold Job Estabrook 2 brooms, at 15 c.; 7 yds. of checked gingham, at 22 c.; $1\frac{3}{4}$ yds. of blue drill, at 16 c.; and delivered to Miss Kelley on his order $7.30 in goods, as per bill rendered.

Tr. 2. Received of Samuel H. Morris 26½ lbs. of wool, at 40 c., and 4 bushels of potatoes, at 35 c.

Tr. 3. Sold to John W. Thomson 10 yds. of calico, at 31 c.; 4 yds. of diaper, at 13 c.; 2 pr. of bl'k cotton gloves, at 31 c.; 3 pr. of white cotton hose, at 25 c.; 4 spools of cotton thread, at 6 c.; 2 pr. of side-combs, at 14 c.; and 2 pr. of thick-soled buskins, at $1.50.

Friday, June 27th, 1851.

Tr. 1. George H. Brewster exchanged a piece of gingham previously purchased, for another worth 56 c. more ; bought 3 yds. of blue drill, at 15 c. ; $3\frac{1}{2}$ yds. of cambric, at 10 c. ; 50 lbs. of brown sugar, at 9 c. ; and 3 galls. of molasses, at 56 c. Received of him 15 lbs. of wool, at 35 c.

Tr. 2. Sold William Eldred 1 set of coffee-cups, for $1.00 ; 1 pr. of gent's gaiters, for $2.25 ; and 6 yds. of stair carpet, at 15 c. Received his accepted order on Stewart & Co., payable the 10th of July, for $25.00, and 18 lbs. of wool, at 30 c.

Saturday, June 28th, 1851.

Received of Lyman Marsh $49\frac{1}{2}$ lbs. of wool, at 40 c. Sold him 2 back-combs, at 25 c. ; 2 yds. of lace, at 40 c. ; 5 yds. of cap ribbon, at 10 c. ; 6 yds. of linen, at $37\frac{1}{2}$ c. ; and a remnant of lawn, for $1.00.

Monday, June 30th, 1851.

Tr. 1. Sold Datus C. Brooks 1 box of blacking, for 6 c. ; 1 brush, for 20 c. ; 1 pr. of suspenders, for 38 c. ; 1 pr. of linen gloves, for 44 c. ; 4 skeins of silk, at 5 c. ; 2 doz. skeins of thread, at 8 c. ; 1 piece of sheeting, containing 41 yds., at 11 c. ; and 10 yds. of blue drill, at $12\frac{1}{2}$ c. Received of him $5.00 in cash, on account.

Tr. 2. Sold John C. Goodale 3 yds. of light cassimere, at $1.75 ; trimmings, for 32 c. ; and 8 yds. of Russia sheeting, at $37\frac{1}{2}$ c.

Tr. 3. Sold Isaac Newton 3 yds. of stripe kersey, at 22 c. ; $\frac{1}{2}$ lb. of black tea, at 75 c. ; and $2\frac{1}{2}$ lbs. of sugar, at 10 c.

Tr. 4. Sold Otis B. Waters $10\frac{1}{2}$ yds. of gingham, at 44 c. ; 2 bed-cords, at 31 c. ; and 1 piece of sheeting, containing $31\frac{1}{2}$ yds., at 10 c.

Tuesday, July 1st, 1851.

Tr. 1. Sold George H. Brewster 3 yds. of Franklin stripe, at 25 c.; 14 yds. of sheeting, at 10 c.; 2 yds. of bleached sheeting, at 16 c.; 2 doz. shirt buttons, at 6 c.; 1 doz. susp. buttons, for 6 c.; and 4 spools of thread, at 6 c.

Tr. 2. Sold William Eldred 2 lbs. of raisins, at $12\frac{1}{2}$ c.; $1\frac{1}{2}$ galls. of molasses, at 56 c.; 2 cards of hooks and eyes, at 6 c.; 8 yds. of stripe shirting, at 14 c.; and $41\frac{1}{2}$ yds. of sheeting, at 10 c.

Tr. 3. Paid Lyman Marsh's hired girl, on his verbal order, $1.25; sold him 2 yds. of cap ribbon, at $12\frac{1}{2}$ c.; and 5 yds. of bleached shirting, at 17 c.

Tr. 4. Sold Datus C. Brooks 1 pail, for 25 c.; 3 lbs. of rope, at 15 c.; let him have 10 c. to pay postage; sold him $31\frac{1}{4}$ yds. of shirting, at 8 c.; 1 broom, at 15 c.; and 1 set of cups and saucers, for 25 c.

Tr. 5. Received of Ira Allen 10 lbs. of butter, at 8 c.; 4 doz. eggs, at 7 c.; and cash to balance his account. How much cash did he pay? *Ans.* $7.02.

Wednesday, July 2d, 1851.

Tr. 1. Sold Datus C. Brooks 4 bowls, at 10 c.; 1 deep dish, for 31 c.; 2 lbs. of saleratus, at 8 c.; 2 galls. of molasses, at 56 c.; $15\frac{1}{2}$ lbs. of sugar, at 10 c.; and 1 broom, for 15 c.

Tr. 2. Sold John C. Goodale 1 pr. of white silk gloves, for 50 c.; 4 yds. of edging, at 10 c.; 9 yds. of bleached shirting, at 16 c.; $\frac{1}{2}$ yd. of linen, at 75 c.; 2 doz. shirt buttons, at 9 c.; and 3 spools of thread, at 6 c.

Tr. 3. Sold Isaac Newton 1 lawn dress pattern, for $4.00; $1\frac{1}{4}$ yds. of blue drill, at 12 c.; 2 cards of hooks and eyes, at 8 c.; and $\frac{1}{2}$ doz. tumblers, at $1.00.

Tr. 4. Settled with Reu Corbett, and received the balance due from him in cash. How much was it? *Ans.* $11.45.

Thursday, July 3d, 1851.

Tr. 1. Sold Otis B. Waters 1 piece of sheeting, containing 38¼ yds., at 11 c.; 10½ lbs. of sugar, at 10 c.; and 1 lb. of saleratus, at 8 c.

Tr. 2. Sold John L. Cady 2 pr. of rubber suspenders, at 31 c.; 2 pocket-knives, at 25 c.; 2 vest patterns, at $1.25; and trimmings, for 35 c.; all of which were delivered to his sons.

Tr. 3. Sold William Loomis 3¼ lbs. of soap, at 7 c.; 1 piece of sheeting, containing 35½ yds., at 10 c.; and 8 bbls. of salt, at $1.25. Settled with him, and received cash to balance his account. What was the amount of cash received on settlement? *Ans.* $3.99.

Monday, July 7th, 1851.

Tr. 1. Sold John C. Norton 2 lbs. of coffee, at 13 c.; 8 lbs. of sugar, at 9½ c.; and ½ lb. saleratus, at 8 c.

Tr. 2. Sold William Eldred 3 yds. of factory gingham, at 16⅔ c.; 1½ doz. button moulds, at 4 c.; 2 skeins of white silk, at 4 c.; 2¾ yds. of edging, at 8 c.; and 2 yds. of cap ribbon, at 9½ c.

Tr. 3. Sold James Harper 2 pr. of youths' shoes, at 50 c., and one piece of brown muslin, containing 30 yds., at 11 c.

Tr. 4. Sold Henry R. Waldron 2 bowls, at 8 c.; 4 lbs. of sugar, at 10 c.; 2 lbs. of coffee, at 12½ c.; 1½ lbs. of saleratus, at 8 c.; and 1 pitcher, for 38 c.

Tr. 5. Sold Benj. E. Holmes 2 deep dishes, at 19 c.; 1 set of knives and forks, for $1.87; 1 pr. of scissors, for 31 c.; 1 dressing-comb, for 13 c.; 1 back-comb, for 9 c.; 23½ lbs. of codfish, at 6¼ c.; and 1 doz. German silver tea-spoons, for $1.75.

Tr. 6. Received of Henry R. Thomas 15 lbs. of butter, at 8 c.; 10 doz. eggs, at 8½ c.; and cash to balance his account. How much cash did he pay? *Ans.* $3.96.

Wednesday, July 9th, 1851.

Tr. 1. Sold William Phelps 1 pr. of white silk gloves, for 50 c.; 3 yds. of pink gingham, at 33⅓ c.; 10 lbs. of corn starch, at 12½ c.; and 18 lbs. of crushed sugar, at 10½ c.

Tr. 2. Sold Job C. Pierson 1¾ yds. of silk, at $1.00; 9 yds. of calico, at 16⅔ c.; 2 yds. of bleached drill, at 12½ c.; and paid John James on his verbal order $2.25.

Tr. 3. Sold John Benson 5 lbs. of sugar, at 10 c.; 6 doz. eggs, at 8 c.; 4 scythe stones, at 10 c.; 7¾ yds. of calico, at 16 c.; 8 lbs. of crushed sugar, at 15 c.; 3½ lbs. of saleratus, at 8 c.; 8¾ lbs. of cheese, at 7 c.; and paid the amount remaining due in cash. What was the amount of cash paid him?

Ans. $0.84.

Friday, July 11th, 1851.

Tr. 1. Received of Job Estabrook 8 doz. eggs. at 8 c., and 10 lbs. of butter, at 9 c.

Tr. 2. Sold Benj. E. Holmes 1 pr. of gent's gaiter boots, for $2.25. Received of him, on account, $2.00 in cash.

Tr. 3. Sold William Phelps 3 yds. of linen, at 18¾ c.; 5 yds. of striped linen, at 31¼ c.; 1½ yds. of ribbon, at 10 c.; and a remnant of ribbon, for 4 c. Received on his account $2.00 in cash.

Tr. 4. Received of Job Estabrook $5.00 in cash on his account, and his note to balance. What was the amount named in the note? -- *Ans.* $13.03.

Saturday, July 12th, 1851.

Tr. 1. Sold Job C. Pierson 6¾ yds. of calico, at 16 c.; 8 yds. of brown drilling, at 12½ c.; 4½ yds. of sheeting, at 10 c.; and 1 bonnet, for girl, for 75 c.

Tr. 2. Sold Andrew Jackson 9 yds. of calico, at 16⅔ c.; 4½ yds. of sheeting, at 10 c.; ½ lb. of black tea, at 75 c.; and 4 lbs.

5* 105

of rice, at 7 c. Received of him 8 qts. of whortleberries, at 8 c., and 2 doz. eggs, at 8 c.

Tr. 3. Sold John Ransom 6 lbs. of brown sugar, at 10 c.; 9 lbs. of crushed sugar, at 15 c.; and 6½ yds. of gingham lawn, at 30 c. Received of him 10 qts. of whortleberries, at 8 c., and 6 qts. of strawberries, at 6 c.

Tr. 4. Sold Samuel H. Morris 3 yds. of Russia sheeting, at 33⅓ c.; 8 lbs. of butter, at 12½ c.; and paid the balance due him on account in cash. How much cash did he receive?

Ans. $2.02.

Monday, July 14th, 1851.

Tr. 1. Paid John Robertson's order for $8.00 to J. Frink; sold him 10 lbs. of brown sugar, at 9 c.; and 4 lbs. of crushed sugar, at 14 c.

Tr. 2. Sold William Eldred 6 yds. of calico, at 15 c.; 9 yds. of calico, at 16⅔ c.; 1¾ yds. of check, at 20 c.; and 1 paper of pins, for 12 c.

Tr. 3. Sold Lyman Marsh 37½ lbs. of butter, at 8 c.; 44 lbs. of sugar, at 9 c.; and 2 gallons of molasses, at 44 c. Received of him a note against N. O. Olds, for $15.00.

Tr. 4. Received of John W. Thomson 10 bushels of potatoes, at 25 c.; $5.00 in cash, on account; and his note to balance, at 3 mos. What was the amount named in the note?

Ans. $14.48.

Friday, July 18th, 1851.

Tr. 1. Sold George H. Brewster 2 oz. of nutmegs, at 12½ c., and 14 yds. of Sea Island sheeting, at 14 c. Received of him 10 lbs. of butter, at 10 c.; 6 qts. of whortleberries, at 8 c.; and 5¼ qts. of strawberries, at 4 c.

Tr. 2. Sold William Eldred 20 yds. of bleached sheeting, at 18¾ c.; 4½ yds. of white flannel, at 56 c.; 1 pr. of white silk gloves, for 50 c.; and 1 pr. of Lisle thread gloves, for 35 c.

Tr. 3. Sold Lyman Marsh 1 yd. of satin vesting, for $3.00; ½ quire of letter paper, at 25 c.; 1 box of mustard, for 12 c.; 1 pr. of kip brogans, for $1.25; 2 bars of soap, at 12 c.; and sundry trimmings,* for $2.21.

Tr. 4. Received of Datus C. Brooks $5.00 in cash, on account, and his note to balance. For what amount was his note given? *Ans.* $4.59.

Monday, July 21st, 1851.

Tr. 1. Received of John C. Goodale 18 lbs. of cheese, at 7 c., and 10 lbs. of butter, at 9 c. Sold him 40 lbs. of sugar, at 9 c.; 4 lbs. of coffee, at 14 c.; and 1 coffee-mill, for 44 c.

Tr. 2. Sold Isaac Newton 1 yd. of black ribbon for hat, for 16 c.; 5 yds. of bleached muslin, at 15 c.; 15 yds. of blea. mus., at 20 c.; ½ lb. of sewing silk, at $10.00; 4 lbs. of cotton batting, at 10 c.; 2 doz. shirt buttons, at 20 c.; and 2 doz. horn buttons, at 8 c.

Tr. 3. Received of George H. Brewster 4 bushels of potatoes, at 30 c.; 8 lbs. of butter, at 10 c.; and cash to balance the account. What was the amount paid in cash? *Ans.* $7.76.

Tuesday, July 29th, 1851.

Tr. 1. Sold Otis B. Waters 1½ gallons of molasses, at 56 c.; 12 lbs. of sugar, at 9½ c.; 6½ lbs. of soap, at 8 c.; and 10 yds. of calico, at 16⅔ c. Received of him 14 bushels of oats, at 25 c.

Tr. 2. Sold Lyman Marsh 12 yds. of bed-ticking, at 25 c.; 8 yds. of calico, at 12½ c.; and paid him the balance remaining due on-account in cash. How much cash did he receive? *Ans.* $2.03.

Thursday, July 31st, 1851.

Tr. 1. Sold John L. Cady 8 lbs. of codfish, at 6¼ c., and 1¾ yds. of silk serge, at $1.60.

---

* See remarks in relation to such charges at the 38th page.

Tr. 2. Sold James Harper 2 bbls. of salt, at $1.25 ; 1 bag of fine salt, for 40 c. ; 1 straw hat, for 38 c. ; and 1 yd. of black ribbon, for 10 c. Received of him $19\frac{6}{16}$ lbs. of butter, at 10 c., and 5 doz. eggs, at 8 c.

Tr. 3. Sold John C. Norton 11 yds. of ticking, at 25 c., and 1 penknife, for 31 c. Received of him 1 dry hide, weighing $21\frac{3}{4}$ lbs., at 5 c., and 10 lbs. of butter, at 9 c.

Tr. 4. Sold William Eldred 1 piece of sheeting, containing $37\frac{1}{2}$ yds., at 10 c.

Tr. 5. Received of John C. Goodale 8 bundles of oat-straw, at 3 c., and cash to balance his account. How much was paid in cash ? *Ans.* $13.85.

Monday, August 4th, 1851.

Tr. 1. Sold Henry Waldron 12 yds. of stripe shirting, at $12\frac{1}{2}$ c. ; $6\frac{3}{4}$ yds. of sheeting, at 9 c. ; 3 spools of thread, at 6 c. ; 1 doz. pearl buttons, for 10 c. ; and 4 doz. bone buttons, at 4 c.

Tr. 2. Sold Benj. E. Holmes 2 lbs. of black tea, at 75 c., and $\frac{1}{2}$ lb. of old Hyson do., at $1.00.

Tr. 3. Sold Andrew Jackson 2 sets of cups and saucers, at $32\frac{1}{2}$ c. ; 1 pr. of kip brogans, for $1.25 ; 1 pr. of slips, for 75 c. ; and $2\frac{3}{4}$ yds. of bl'k cassimere, at $2.00.

Tuesday, August 5th, 1851.

Tr. 1. Received of John Robertson, on account, $5.00 in cash.

Tr. 2. Sold Otis B. Waters 8 yds. of bl'k calico, at 14 c., and 20 lbs. of sugar, at 9 c. Received of him, on account, $2.00 in cash, and his note to balance. What was the amount named in the note ? *Ans.* $15.32.

Wednesday, August 6th, 1851.

Tr. 1. Sold William Eldred 9 yds. of gingham, at $37\frac{1}{2}$ c. ; 1 yd. of bleached drill, for 12 c. ; $1\frac{1}{2}$ yds. of calico, at 10 c. ; and 1 card of hooks and eyes, for 9 c.

Tr. 2. Sold John L. Cady 1 gall. of molasses, for 50 c.; 4½ lbs. of sugar, at 10 c.; and 6 qts. of berries, at 4 c.

Tr. 3. Sold Isaac Newton 6 doz. eggs, at 8 c., and 7 lbs. of butter, at 10 c. Settled the account, and received the balance due in cash. What was the amount of cash received?

Ans. $17.15.

Friday, August 8th, 1851.

Tr. 1. Sold Benj. E. Holmes ¼ bushel of whortleberries, at $1.50 ; 1 straw hat, for 37 c.; and 1 ribbon for hat, for 10 c.

Tr. 2. Paid Job C. Pierson's order for $2.00 ; sold him 1 bbl. of flour, for $4.50 ; and 6 bbls. of salt, at $1.25.

Tr. 3. Sold Andrew Jackson 1 pr. of thick boots, (as they are,*) for $1.75 ; 1 straw hat, for 38 c.; 1 yd. of ribbon, for 6 c.; and 2 cards of hooks and eyes, at 9 c.

Tr. 4. Sold John Robertson 23 qts. of whortleberries, at 4 c.; 1 pr. of white cotton hose, for 38 c.; 1 straw hat, for 12 c.; 5 lbs. of sugar, at 10 c.; and ½ lb. of corn starch, at 12 c.

Tr. 5. Received of William Eldred 26½ lbs. of butter, at 10 c., and cash to balance his account. How much was paid in cash?

Ans. $8.54.

Saturday, August 9th, 1851.

Tr. 1. Sold William Phelps 1⅜ yds. of blue cloth, at $3.50, and 3 skeins of silk and twist, at 5 c.

Tr. 2. Sold John Ransom 4 lbs. of candles, at 10½ c.; 4 boxes of matches, at 4 c.; and paid two of his orders, one for $1.50, and the other for $2.25.

Tr. 3. Sold James Harper 1 pr. of linen gloves, for 44 c.; 1 pr. of suspenders, for 50 c.; and 12 qts. of whortleberries, at 4 c. Settled, and received the balance due in cash. What was the amount of cash received?

Ans. $6.76.

---

* The boots were damaged, and were sold as such.

Tuesday, August 12th, 1851.

Tr. 1. Sold John C. Norton ½ quire of letter paper, at 20 c., and 2 lbs. of raisins, at 9 c.

Tr. 2. Sold Henry R. Waldron 1½ yds. of white flannel, at 50 c.; 1½ yds. of red flannel, at 44 c.; 1 set of knitting pins, for 8 c.; and 8 yds. of tow cloth, at 20 c.

Tr. 3. Sold John Robertson 10 yds. of gingham, at 37½ c., and 1 straw hat and ribbon, for 75 c.

Tr. 4. Sold John C. Norton 1 set of cups and saucers, for 50 c., and 3½ yds. of bleached muslin, at 20 c. Received the balance due on account in cash. What was the amount paid in cash? *Ans.* $3.61.

Wednesday, August 13th, 1851.

Tr. 1. Sold John L. Cady 1½ yds. of blue cloth, at $3.50; trimmings for pants, for 61 c.; and 9¾ yds. stripe shirting, at 15 c. Received of him an accepted order on Job Orr, for $10.00.

Tr. 2. Sold Benj. E. Holmes 1 bbl. of salt, for $1.25, and sundries for Susan, per verbal order, amounting to 37 c.

Tr. 3. Sold Job C. Pierson 1 wood pail, for 25 c.; 10½ lbs. of sugar, at 10 c.; 5 lbs. of coffee, at 12½ c.; and 7 lbs. of candles, at 12½ c.

Tr. 4. Sold Andrew Jackson 2 lbs. of saleratus, at 8 c., and 8 lbs. of crushed sugar, at 15 c. Settled, and received the balance in cash. What was the amount of cash paid on settlement? *Ans.* $13.69.

Thursday, August 14th, 1851.

Tr. 1. Sold John Ransom 2½ yds. black cassimere, at $1.56, and trimmings for pants, for 44 c.

Tr. 2. Sold John Robertson 1 pocket-knife, for 50 c., and ½ lb. of starch, at 12 c.

Tr. 3. Sold William Phelps 1 doz. blue plates, for $1.00, and 2 sets of cups and saucers, at 50 c. Settled, and received his note, at 30 days, to balance the account. For what amount was his note given?   *Ans.* $11.91.

Friday, August 15th, 1851.

Tr. 1. Received of John L. Cady the balance due on his account in cash. What was the amount paid?   *Ans.* $5.78.

Tr. 2. Received of Henry R. Waldron the balance due on his account in cash. What was the amount paid?
Ans. $6.95.

Tr. 3. Settled with Benj. E. Holmes, and received his note, at 30 days, to balance the account. For what amount was his note given?   *Ans.* $10.72.

Saturday, August 16th, 1851.

Tr. 1. Sold Job C. Pierson 1 white pitcher, for 16 c.; 3 bowls, at 8 c.; 2 tumblers, at 7 c.; one set of cups and saucers, for 25 c.; stone-ware, for 53 c.; and $\frac{1}{2}$ lb. of crushed sugar, at 14 c.

Tr. 2. Sold John Robertson 1 pocket-knife, for 38 c.; 9 yds. of gingham, at $37\frac{1}{2}$ c.; and 3 yds. of blue calico, at $12\frac{1}{2}$ c. Received $25\frac{1}{2}$ lbs. of butter, at 10 c.

Monday, August 25th, 1851.

Sold Job C. Pierson 3 yds. of stripe cassimere, at $1.25, and trimmings for pants, for 57 c.

Monday, September 1st, 1851.

Settled with Job C. Pierson, and received the amount due in cash. How much was it?   *Ans.* $31.54.

Wednesday, September 3d, 1851.

Tr. 1.   Settled with John Ransom, and received his note to balance the account.   For what amount was his note given?
Ans. $11.41.

Tr. 2.   Settled with John Robertson.   Received $5.00 in cash, and his due-bill to balance the account.   For what sum was his due-bill given?   *Ans.* $8.08.

AUXILIARY BOOKS.

It has already been stated that in the Third Form of Accounts there are two principal books—the Day-book and the Ledger. See page 80th.

AUXILIARY BOOKS are assisting or helping books.   The most important of these are—the Cash-book, the Bill-book, and the Memorandum-book, which have already been described; to which may be added the Letter-book and the Invoice-book.

The CASH-BOOK is a book in which is kept an account of all moneys received, and of all moneys paid out.   For the manner of keeping it, see pages 34–35.   When the Cash-book contains entries that require to be posted into the Ledger, the instructions should be observed that have already been given for posting from the Day-book into the Ledger.   See p. 82d.

The BILL-BOOK is a book in which a person keeps an account of his notes, bills receivable, bills payable, and bills of exchange. For a fuller description of it, and the manner of keeping it, see pages 44–47.

The MEMORANDUM-BOOK is used for recording memorandums of various kinds, agreements, and all important particulars relating to a person's business that belong neither to the Day-book nor Ledger.   For a more full description of it, and the manner of keeping it, see pages 49–53.

What are the two principal books in the third form of accounts? What are Auxiliary Books?   What are the most important of them?   What is the Cash-book?   What is the Bill-book?   For what is the Memorandum-book used?

The LETTER-BOOK contains copies of all business letters, which ought always to be written in a neat and legible hand, and to be as clear and concise as possible. By using a copying machine much labor may be saved in keeping this book, and at the same time perfect accuracy secured.

Good letter-writing is a fine accomplishment. The following specimen is therefore subjoined for the purpose of exhibiting the date (1), address (2), body of the letter (3), subscription (4), inscription (5), and superscription (6).

LETTER OF INTRODUCTION.

(1) *Philadelphia, July 25th, 1851.*

(2) *Gentlemen:*

(3) *Allow me to introduce to your honorable house my young friend, Timothy Trusty, of this city, who visits New York for the purpose of procuring a situation in a Book-Publishing Establishment. From a knowledge of his uniform kindness and obedience as a son; of his industry and attainments as a student; of his proverbial honesty and truthfulness; and of his many amiable qualities, I think him such a person as you will be pleased to employ, in case you need additional help; and I therefore take great pleasure in introducing him to your favorable acquaintance.*

(4) *I remain, Gentlemen,*

Yours, very respectfully,

(5) *Messrs. Cady & Burgess,* *Samuel Peabody.*
New York.

What does the Letter-book contain? How ought letters to be written? What of a copying machine? What is said of good letter-writing? For what purpose is a specimen of letter-writing introduced? Do the traits of character attributed to the person described in this letter of introduction entitle him to confidence and esteem? What are some of these traits of character?

Below is exhibited the correct form of a letter when folded. The superscription (6) should occupy the lower half of the letter, both on account of its appearance, and the convenience of post-marking at the office. Postage is generally *pre-paid* under the present law.

(6) *Messrs. Cady & Burgess,*

No. 60 John Street,

New York.

The INVOICE-BOOK is a book kept by many merchants, into which are copied all *invoices*, or bills of goods purchased. But this requires much labor in copying, and is really of little use; for in case of any difficulty with the seller, it is necessary to refer to *his own list*, and not to a copy of it. Invoices should be carefully compared with the goods actually received, so that in case of disagreement any error may be corrected, and then placed on file for future reference, as occasion shall require. When found correct, they should be entered in the Day-book, to the credit of the person of whom the goods have been received, as in case of credits per bill, described at the 38th and 39th pages.

BOOKS OF ACCOUNT.

Persons are sometimes allowed to introduce their books of account as evidence in their favor; but such testimony is always

---

What is the Invoice-book? Does this require much labor? Why is it of little use? What should be done with Invoices? When found correct, where should they be entered? Are books of account ever received as evidence? To what is such testimony liable?

liable to the strictest scrutiny. A person who would introduce his own books as testimony in his favor in court, must be able to prove, by those who have dealt with him and settled their accounts, that he keeps his books correctly and honestly. He must also prove that the books produced are his account-books, and that some of the articles charged have been delivered.

NOTES, ORDERS, AND RECEIPTS.

A NOTE is a written or printed paper acknowledging a debt and promising payment.

A PROMISSORY NOTE, called also a Note of Hand, is a writing which contains a promise of the payment of money or the delivery of property to another, at or before a time specified, in consideration of value received by the promiser, or person who signs the note. The terms, *maker* of a note, and *payee* of a note, are defined at the 45th page, which see.

A NEGOTIABLE NOTE is one that may be transferred from one person to another, or that may be bought and sold, and thus have different owners at different times. Notes are usually made payable to the payee or *his order ;* to the payee or *the bearer ;* or simply to *the bearer.* All such notes are *negotiable ;* but when a note that has been given to the payee or *his order* is transferred, the payee must *indorse* it by writing his own name upon the back of it. The collection of a note that is made payable to a specified person, without any mention of *his order,* or *the bearer,* can be enforced by the payee only, or by his legal representatives. Such notes are *not* negotiable.

A DUE-BILL is a written promise to pay a certain sum of money, or a specified amount in goods or property, to a person

What must a person who would introduce his books as testimony be able to prove? What is a Note? What is a *Promissory* Note? Who is the *maker*, and who the *payee* of a note? What is a *negotiable* note? To whom are notes usually made payable? Are such notes *negotiable?* When must a note be *indorsed?* What notes can be collected by the payee only, or by his legal representatives? Are such notes *negotiable?* What is a Due-bill?

115

named, to his order, or to the bearer. Due-bills are notes, though less formal than promissory notes usually are. Whether negotiable or not, depends upon the circumstances just enumerated.

A BANK-NOTE is a promissory note, issued by a banking company, signed by the president and countersigned by the cashier, payable to the bearer in gold or silver at the bank, on demand. Bank-notes are of course negotiable, being made payable to *the bearer*.

An ORDER is a written request to deliver money, goods, or other property, to some person specified, to his order, or to the bearer. The person on whom an order may be given is under no legal obligations to pay it, unless he first engages to do so. Orders are generally considered payable on presentation. They are sometimes *accepted* by the person on whom they are drawn. This may be done by his simply writing the word "*Accepted*" either across the back or face of the order, (but usually the latter, and in red ink,) and signing his name to it. Before this is done, an order may be regarded as evidence of debt against the *drawer* of it; but afterward, it may be considered as evidence of debt against the *accepter*.

A RECEIPT is a written statement, signed by the giver of it, acknowledging that he has received a specified amount of money, goods, or other property. A receipt of money may be in part or in full payment of a debt, and it operates as a discharge of the debt either in part or in full, as the case may be. A receipt of goods makes the receiver liable to account for the same, according to the nature of the transaction, or the tenor of the writing. Orders and receipts, like bills of goods, should be preserved and placed on file.

Are due-bills notes? Are they *negotiable*? What is a Bank-note? Are Bank-notes negotiable? What is an Order? Is the person on whom an order may be drawn under obligations to pay it? When are orders generally considered payable? How may an order be accepted by the person upon whom it is drawn? Against whom may an order be considered as evidence of debt? What is a Receipt? How does a receipt of money operate? How a receipt of goods? What should be done with orders and receipts?

EXAMPLES OF NOTES, ORDERS, AND RECEIPTS.

Example 1st.—A Promissory Note.

$45.50.

Thirty days after date, I promise to pay Samuel Bronson, or Order, at my store in Brooklyn, forty-five and $\frac{50}{100}$ dollars, value received.

Henry Paywell.

Brooklyn, September 1st, 1851.

This note is *negotiable,* but needs to be *indorsed* by Samuel Bronson, if it passes from his hands.

Example 2d.—A common Note of Hand.

$24.00.

For value received, I promise to pay Ira Merchant, or Bearer, twenty-four dollars, the tenth day of July, 1852, with interest from the tenth of January next.

Timothy Truthful.

Washington, September 10th, 1851.

Example 3d.—A Note for Property.

Whiteford, May 10th, 1851.

Sixty days after date, I promise to deliver to John Burch, or Order, at my wagon-shop in Whiteford, a good one-horse wagon, worth sixty dollars.

Samuel White.

Example 4th.—A Due-bill for Goods.

$14.25.

Due Henry Whitcomb, or Order, fourteen and $\frac{25}{100}$ dollars in goods from my store, value received.

John H. Whipple.

Adams, June 20th, 1851.

Example 5th.—An Order for Money and Goods.

Monroe, July 25th, 1851.

James Armitage, Esq.

Please pay to William Faithful, or Order, fourteen dollars in goods from your store, and six dollars in money, and charge the same to

$20.00.   Smith & Whitney.

Example 6th.—A Receipt for Property.

Received, Whiteford, July 1st, 1851, of Samuel White, a good one-horse wagon, in full of his agreement of May 10th, 1851.   John Burch.

Example 7th.—A Receipt in full of all Demands.

$217.17.

Received from James Mitchell, per Job Willson, two hundred and seventeen and $\frac{17}{100}$ dollars, in full of all demands.   Kingsley & Bingham.

New York, July 10th, 1851.

DOUBLE ENTRY BOOK-KEEPING.

THIS is a system of Book-keeping in which every transaction is *twice entered;* first on the Dr. side of one account, and then on the Cr. side of some other account to which it also belongs. It is from this circumstance that it derives its name. Double Entry is especially adapted to the wants of persons engaged in a wholesale trade, or in any business which is complicated.

In Double Entry Book-keeping three principal books are generally employed, viz., a Blotter or Day-book, a Journal, and a Ledger. But many of our best book-keepers now dispense with the use of one of these books, and thereby save to themselves much time and labor in writing. In this treatise the Journal and Ledger only are used. This frequently requires an additional line between the Dr. and Cr. entries in the Journal, showing where the sum or sums entered may be found, or on what account they have been received or paid. These references are generally made either to the Invoice-book, (see entries *2, 6, and 8 in the Journal,) or to the Sales-book, (see entries 3, 4, 5— 9, 11, 12, etc.) When not to one of these, the nature of the transaction will suggest the proper reference phrase.

* By referring to the entries in the Journal it will be seen that they are numbered in full-faced figures. This has been done in order to facilitate the reference to particular entries in giving explanations of the mode of making the Journal entries, of posting them to their proper accounts in the Ledger, and of balancing the accounts.

What is Double Entry Book-keeping? To whose wants is it especially adapted? How many principal books are generally kept in double entry, and what are they? With what do many of our best book-keepers now dispense? In this treatise what books only are used? For what purpose is an additional line in the Journal frequently required? To what books are these references generally made?

DEFINITION OF BOOKS.

The INVOICE-BOOK is a book in which are entered at length all *invoices*, or bills of goods *purchased*. It may be made by pasting the original invoices into a book made of coarse paper for that purpose. When invoices are numbered and placed on file, as recommended at the 114th page, they may be referred to by number, as in the Examples for Practice, page 140th.

The SALES-BOOK is a book in which are entered at length all bills of merchandise *sold*. It is kept much like the Day-book.

The JOURNAL either contains the particulars of every business transaction, or it makes special reference to the name and page of the book in which they may be found, or if to papers on file, to their title and number. In it the entries are so recorded that they may be readily posted to their proper accounts in the Ledger. It is ruled like the Day-book in the third form of accounts, with this exception—it contains two sets of money columns. The Dr. sums are all entered in the left-hand columns, and the Cr. sums in the right-hand columns. In case there are several Dr. items in an entry, to be posted to as many different accounts, their sum will exactly equal the Cr. entry, and vice versa. In such cases it is customary to use the word "Sundries" before the several particulars that are entered at the Dr. side of the account, as in entries **1, 6,** and **28,** in the Journal. In entries **19** and **26** the reverse is true, the Dr. entries being posted to one account, and the Cr. entries each to *sundry* accounts. The word "Sundries," however, in such cases, although sometimes employed, is not used in the annexed Journal.

What is the Invoice-book? How may it be made? When invoices are numbered and placed on file, how may they be referred to? What is the Sales-book? What does the Journal contain? How are the entries recorded in it? How is it ruled? Where are the Dr. sums entered, and where the Cr. sums? When there are several Dr. items in an entry to be posted to as many different accounts, what will their sum exactly equal? What of the word "Sundries" in such cases? When there is one Dr. sum in an entry, and several Cr. items to be posted against it, is the word "Sundries" then used?

In all cases the Dr. amount posted from an entry, whether to one or more accounts, should exactly equal the Cr. amount. The general principle is beautifully illustrated in the symbol of a pair of scales on the title-page of the Book-keeping. The symbol on the title-page of the Account-books particularly illustrates entry 1 in the Journal.

When a page of the Journal has been written up, the money columns should be footed, and in case the Dr. and Cr. amounts exactly agree, the inference is that the sums have been correctly entered. If they disagree, it is certain a mistake has been made. The work should then be carefully reviewed, and all errors corrected, as directed at the 83d page.

Rules for Journalizing have in numerous instances been carefully drawn up to aid the learner in making his Journal entries. Of the many rules that might be given, none, perhaps, are superior to the following, which may be the better remembered for being expressed in homely verse.

> "By Journal laws what you receive
> Is Debtor made to what you give.
> Stock for your debts must Debtor be,
> And Creditor for property.
> Profit and Loss Accounts are plain;
> You debit Loss and credit Gain."

The Ledger in Double Entry Book-keeping, like that already described, is a book to which the entries recorded in the Journal are transferred and so arranged as to present each account on a folio by itself. The instructions given in relation to the Ledger and Posting Books, at the 81st and 82d pages, are applicable here. The letter *J*, in the Ledger, stands for Journal.

To what is the Dr. amount posted from an entry in all cases equal? What symbol illustrates the general principle? What symbol particularly illustrates the first entry in the Journal? How may you determine whether the Journal entries on a page have been correctly made? When is it certain a mistake has been made? Give the rule for making Journal entries. What is the Ledger? For what does *J* stand?

CLASSES OF ACCOUNTS.

The accounts in a merchant's Ledger may be classified under the three following heads—Real Accounts, Personal Accounts, and Imaginary Accounts.

REAL ACCOUNTS include all accounts of effects or things which a person possesses. Of this class are the Cash Account and the Merchandise Account. To these might be added the several accounts kept in the First and Second Forms of Account, other than accounts with persons; such as the Cornfield Account, the Account with a Field of Oats, the Beef Account, the Sheep and Wool Account, the Tobacco Account, and the Winebibber's Account.

PERSONAL ACCOUNTS are the accounts kept with different persons with whom we deal.

IMAGINARY ACCOUNTS are fictitious titles invented to represent the person or company that conduct a business, or to supply the want of some real or personal titles in recording such gains or losses as cannot with propriety be placed to Real or Personal Accounts. Of this class are the Stock Account, the Profit and Loss Account, the Expense Account, and the Balance Account.

TITLES OF ACCOUNTS.

The STOCK ACCOUNT represents the person or company that conduct the business. On the Dr. side of this account are entered all the sums they owe on commencing business, and on the Cr. side the amount of money and the value of property they carry into business. The excess of the credits over the debits will be the *net* amount of property invested.

Under how many heads may the accounts in a merchant's Ledger be classified, and what are they? What are Real Accounts? Mention some accounts of this class. What are Personal Accounts? What are Imaginary Accounts? Mention some accounts of this class. What does the Stock Account represent? What sums are entered on the Dr. and what on the Cr. side of this account? How do we arrive at the *net* amount of property invested?

The MERCHANDISE ACCOUNT shows how much has been paid for Merchandise, and how much it has been sold for. On the Dr. side of this account is entered the value of all the Merchandise on hand at the time of commencing business, and the amount paid for all subsequent purchases. On the Cr. side of the account is entered the amount of all sales. In case the Merchandise is all sold, the difference between the Dr. and the Cr. sides of the account will exhibit the gain or loss on Merchandise. If any goods remain unsold, their value should be ascertained by taking an inventory of them, and then be entered on the Cr. side of the account. The mode of doing this and of ascertaining the gross amount of profits in trade, and finally the *net gain*, is shown under the head of Balancing Accounts.

The EXPENSE ACCOUNT includes all sums that have been paid for carrying on one's business; such as freight, clerk hire, store rent, etc. All such expenses should be entered on the Dr. side of this account. The Cr. side of this account contains nothing until the closing of the books. The sum necessary to balance is then entered on the Cr. side, the same amount being likewise entered on the Dr. side of the Profit and Loss Account, as is fully explained under the head of Balancing Accounts, further on.

The CASH ACCOUNT exhibits the receipts and disbursements of Cash, including specie and bank-notes. Although this account is kept in the Ledger, a separate Cash Account is also kept at the 133d page, made up from the Journal entries, which exhibits the same result, as may be seen by comparing the two accounts.

The PROFIT AND LOSS ACCOUNT, as its title implies, is kept to show the Profit or Loss in one's business. On the Dr. side

What does the Merchandise Account show? What entries are made on the Dr. and what on the Cr. side of this account? How is the gain or loss on Merchandise ascertained? What does the Expense Account include? On which side of the account are all expenses entered? What does the Cr. side of this account contain? What does the Cash Account exhibit? Is this account twice presented? Is the result in both cases the same?

of this account are entered all the losses sustained, and all moneys paid for labor, taxes, etc., including the sum necessary to balance the Expense Account. On the Cr. side are entered all gains of whatever kind arising from one's business.

On closing this account, if the sum of the Cr. entries is *greater* than that of the Dr. entries, the difference will be the amount of Profit arising from the business; but if it is *less*, it will exhibit the amount of Loss sustained. In the former instance the account is closed by entering on the debit side the amount necessary to balance, and passing the same sum to the credit of Stock; in the latter, by crediting Profit and Loss and debiting Stock.

The BALANCE ACCOUNT is the title of an account introduced for the purpose of balancing the unclosed accounts, hence its name. Many merchants do not open this account in the Ledger, but confine it to a separate sheet, like the Trial Balance. Such a Balance is exhibited at the 138th page, beneath the Trial Balance.

POSTING BOOKS.

The instructions for Posting Books, given at the 82d page, are applicable here. Every sum entered in the Dr. columns of the Journal is posted into the Ledger to the Dr. side of the account opposite which it stands in the Journal; and every sum entered in the Cr. columns of the Journal is posted to the Cr. side of the account opposite whose title it stands. The reference figures from the page of each book to the page of the other are entered according to the instructions already referred to. The Journal page is entered in the Ledger at the left of

---

For what purpose is the Profit and Loss Account kept? What entries are made on the Dr. and what on the Cr. side of this account? When does this account represent that a Profit has arisen in business, and when that a Loss has been sustained? How is this account closed? What is the Balance Account? Is this account always opened in the Ledger? How are entries posted from the Journal to the Ledger

the money columns into which the sum has been posted, and the Ledger page is entered in the Journal opposite the title of the account that has been posted.

When the Journal entries have been posted to entry **21,** inclusive, and the work has been reviewed and the examining sign affixed, (see p. 81,) a Trial Balance should be taken.

TRIAL BALANCE,

We have already shown how errors may be detected in the Journal entries by adding the sums in the money columns. The Trial Balance, which is taken for the purpose of ascertaining whether the Journal entries have been correctly transferred to the Ledger, as well as to prepare the way for balancing the unclosed accounts, affords a similar test of the accuracy of the posting. Neither test, however, is infallible ; for although the *right sums* may be entered, and in the *right columns,* still they may be entered to the *wrong accounts.* Hence the necessity of constantly exercising great care.

The Trial Balance is taken as follows : First rule a sheet of paper like the Trial Balance given at the 138th page, with money columns at the left and right for Dr. and Cr. entries, and with the necessary space between for entering the titles of the various accounts. Then the two sides of every account in the Ledger should be added, and the less amount subtracted from the greater. All those accounts which will exactly balance should be ruled off and closed at once, and the titles of the unclosed accounts should be entered in the Trial Balance between the money columns. The difference between the footings of the Dr. and Cr. columns of the unclosed accounts should be entered opposite the titles of their accounts respectively ; in the Dr. columns when the debit side of the account is the largest, and in the Cr. columns when the credit side of the account is the largest. Then, as the sum total of the debit entries posted into the Ledger is- exactly equal to the sum of all the credit entries thus posted, and as we have only left off from the Trial Balance those accounts that exactly balance, it is apparent that the sum of all the entries in the Dr. columns should agree with the sum of all the entries in the Cr. columns. The sums in these columns should next be added. In case the footings agree, the inference is that the Journal entries have been correctly posted into the Ledger. If they disagree, it is certain a mistake has been made, and the work should be reviewed.

BALANCING ACCOUNTS.

An Inventory of the Merchandise on hand should now be taken, when we may proceed to balance the unclosed accounts. The Inventory (which in the present case is fictitious) shows that

We have on hand Merchandise to the value of $1,387.64

We have sold, as per Cr. side Mdse. Acct., 12,648.95

Total Cr. to Merchandise Account, 14,036.59

We have paid for Merchandise, 11,506.80

Balance, Gross Profits on Merchandise, 2,529.79

The proper entry is now made in the Journal (**22**), which exhibits the gross amount of profits in trade for six months, and opens an account with Profit and Loss. The next entry (**23**) when posted, closes the Expense Account. Entry **24,** when posted, closes the Profit and Loss Account, and exhibits the *net gain in trade* for six months. Entry **25** exhibits the net value of Stock at the end of six months, and when posted closes that

---

The Trial Balance being completed, what remains to be done before proceeding to balance the unclosed accounts? How do we arrive at the proper sum to insert in entry **22,** and what does the amount there entered exhibit? What is entry **23,** and what its effect when posted? What is entry **24,** and its effect? What entry **25,** and its effect?

account and opens the Balance Account. Entry **26,** when posted, closes the Balance Account and exhibits the true state of our affairs, as set forth in the Balance at the 138th page. Entry **27,** when posted, reopens the Balance Account and closes the Stock Account. Entry **28,** when posted, again closes the Balance Account and reopens all the unsettled accounts.

Entries **27** and **28,** it will be observed, are the reverse of entries **25** and **26.** The accounts whose titles are entered in the Ledger, however, have now all been closed, and those that remain unsettled have been reopened, thus reaching more satisfactorily the results stated in the Balance already referred to.

In closing a set of books, all expenses incurred in carrying on business, together with all gains and losses, should first be brought into the Profit and Loss Account; Profit and Loss should then be closed by Stock; and, finally, all unclosed accounts should first be balanced, and then reopened by the Balance Account.

In the Double Entry Ledger *J*, as has already been intimated, stands for Journal. The *To* and *By*, which are the usual signs of Dr. and Cr. entries, are understood, as they often are in both Journal and Ledger. When a Blotter or Day-book is used, the Journal entry frequently occupies but a single line, thus:

S. C. Woodward & Co. to Bills Payable.

In such cases two columns are required at the left for post marks; the one at the extreme left for the Dr. entries, and the other for the Cr. entries. In all other respects the Posting should be conducted as from the following Journal to the Ledger.

What entry **26,** and its effect? What entry **27,** and its effect? What entry **28,** and its effect? What relation do entries **27** and **28** sustain to entries **25** and **26**? In what condition do they leave the accounts whose titles are entered in the Ledger? In closing a set of books, what order is named for balancing the several accounts? In the Double Entry, what does *J* stand for? What of *To* and *By*? When are two columns required for post marks? What of the Posting in other respects?

JOURNAL A.—DOUBLE ENTRY.

Tuesday, April 1st, 1851.

			Dr.			Cr.	
	Sundries	Dr.					
1	Merchandise, in Store		6600	00			
2	Cash		4500	00			
3	Bills Receivable						
	Note against John Otis,						
	Due July 2d, 1851		3500	00			
1 1	To Stock					14600	00
	— // —						
1	Stock	Dr.					
	Invoice Book A, p. 40		4600	00			
2 2	To Hill & Wright					4600	00
	— April 15th. —						
3	S. C. Woodward & Co.	Dr.					
	Sales Book A, p. 80		1250	00			
1 3	To Merchandise					1250	00
	— May 2d. —						
3	Clark & Smith	Dr.					
	Sales Book A, p. 95		980	50			
1 4	To Merchandise					980	50
	— May 15th. —						
3	Jas. Armitage	Dr.					
	Sales Book A, p. 112		2106	00			
1 5	To Merchandise					2106	00
			23536	50		23536	50

128

	Sundries	Dr.				
1	Merchandise					
	Invoice Book A, p. 60		3480	00		
1	Expenses					
	To N. York for Goods $30.50					
	For Freight on do. 65.50		96	00		
2	6 To Cash				3576	00
	—— June 24th. ——					
1	Cash	Dr.				
	In full of their Acct.		1250	00		
3	7 To S. C. Woodward & Co.				1250	00
	—— " ——					
1	Merchandise	Dr.				
	Invoice Book A, p. 55		1426	80		
2	8 To Cash				1426	80
	—— June 25th. ——					
2	Cash	Dr.				
	Sales Book A, p. 120		547	25		
1	9 To Merchandise				547	25
	—— July 2d. ——					
2	Cash	Dr.				
	On J. Otis Note		3165	40		
3	10 To Bills Receivable				3165	40
	—— July 21st. ——					
3	Clark & Smith	Dr.				
	Sales Book A, p. 132		1275	60		
1	11 To Merchandise				1275	60
			11241	05	11241	05

6*

Wednesday, August 5th, 1851.

3	Jas. Armitage	Dr.		482	75		
1	12	To Merchandise				482	75
		//					
2	Cash	Dr.		2256	10		
3	13	To Clark & Smith				2256	10
	August 6th.						
2	Hill & Wright	Dr.		3420	00		
2	14	To Cash				3420	00
	August 14th.						
1	Expenses	Dr.					
	Paid for Daily Tribune,						
	Six Months	$3.00					
	For Journal of Com.						
	Six Months	5.00	8	00			
2	15	To Cash				8	00
	August 25th.						
3	S. C. Woodward & Co.	Dr.		2280	00		
1	16	To Merchandise				2280	00
	August 27th.						
3	Bills Receivable	Dr.		1912	45		
1	17	To Merchandise				1912	45
				10359	30	10359	30

3	Clark & Smith	Dr.	1814	40			
	Sales Book B p. 28						
1	**18** To Merchandise				1814	40	

———— September 30th. ————

2	Cash	Dr.	4835	80			
	In full of his Acct.						
3	To Jas. Armitage				2588	75	
3	Of J. Otis on Note						
	19 To Bills Receivable				2247	05	

———— " ————

2	Hill & Wright	Dr.	1180	00			
	In full of their Acct.						
2	**20** To Cash				1180	00	

———— " ————

1	Expenses	Dr.					
	Clerk Hire, Job Orr, 6 mos.						
	@ $40.00 $240.00						
	Store Rent 600.00		840	00			
2	**21** To Cash				840	00	

———— " ————

1	Merchandise	Dr.					
	Gross Profits 6 mos.		2529	79			
2	**22** To Profit & Loss				2529	79	

———— " ————

2	Profit & Loss	Dr.					
	Business Expenses 6 mos.		944	00			
1	**23** To Expenses				944	00	

12143	99	12143	99

131

Tuesday, September 30th, 1851.

2	Profit & Loss	Dr.					
	Net Gain in 6 mos.		1585	79			
1	24	To Stock			1585	79	
		//					
1	Stock	Dr.					
	Net Value of Stock		11585	79			
2	25	To Balance			11585	79	
		//					
2	Balance	Dr.	11585	79			
1	To Mdse. per Inventory				1387	64	
2	// Cash				6103	75	
3	. // S. C. Woodward & Co.				2280	00	
3	26 // Clark & Smith				1814	40	
		//					
2	Balance	Dr.					
	Net Value of Stock		11585	79			
1	27	To Stock			11585	79	
		//					
	Sundries	Dr.					
1	Merchandise		1387	64			
2	Cash		6103	75			
3	S. C. Woodward & Co.		2280	00			
3	Clark & Smith		1814	40			
2	28	To Balance			11585	79	
			47928	95	47928	95	

Cash Account. Dr. Cr.

1851				Dr.		Cr.	
Apr.	1	To Balance on hand		4500	00		
June	2	By Am't paid for Mdse.				3480	00
"	"	" Expenses to N. York				30	50
"	"	" Freight on Mdse.				65	50
"	24	To Received of S. C. Woodward & Co.		1250	00		
"	"	By Am't paid for Mdse.				1426	80
"	25	To Rec'd for Mdse.		547	25		
July	2	" " on J. Otis' Note		3165	40		
Aug.	5	" " of Clark & Smith		2256	10		
"	6	By Paid Hill & Wright				3420	00
"	14	" " for Daily Tribune				3	00
"	"	" " for Jour. of Com.				5	00
Sept.	30	To Rec'd of Jas. Armitage		2588	75		
"	"	" " of J. Otis on Note		2247	05		
"	"	By Paid Hill & Wright				1180	00
"	"	" " Job Orr, Clerk				240	00
"	"	" " for Store Rent				600	00
"	"	" Amount on hand				6103	75
				16554	55	16554	55
		To Balance brought down		6103	75		

133

A		H	
Armitage, Jas.	3	Hill & Wright	2

B		I J K	
Balance	2		
Bills Receivable	3		

C		L M	
Cash	2	Merchandise	1
Clark & Smith	3		

D		N O P	
		Profit & Loss	2

E		Q R	
Expenses	1		

F		S T	

G		U V W	
		Woodward, S. C. & Co.	3

1851						1851					
Apr.	1	J.	1	4600	00	Apr.	1	J.	1	14600	00
Sept.	30	''	5	11585	79	Sept.	30	''	5	1585	79
				16185	79					16185	79
						Sept.	30	J.	5	11585	79

Dr.   Merchandise   Cr.

1851						1851					
Apr.	1	J.	1	6600	00	Apr.	15	J.	1	1250	00
June	2	'	2	3480	00	May	2	''	1	980	50
''	24	''	2	1426	80	''	15	''	1	2106	00
Sept.	30	''	4	2529	79	June	25	''	2	547	25
						July	21	''	2	1275	60
						Aug.	5	''	3	482	75
						''	25	''	3	2280	00
						''	27	''	3	1912	45
						Sept.	10	''	4	1814	40
						''	30	''	5	1387	64
				14036	59					14036	59
Sept.	30	J.	5	1387	64						

Dr.   Expenses   Cr.

1851						1851					
June	2	J.	2	96	00	Sept.	30	J.	4	944	00
Aug.	14	''	3	8	00						
Sept.	30	''	4	840	00						
				944	00					944	00

Dr. | Cash | **Cr.**

1851						1851						
Apr.	1	J.	1	4500	00	May	2	J.	2	3576	00
June	24	//	2	1250	00	June	24	//	2	1426	80
//	25	//	2	547	25	Aug.	6	//	3	3420	00
July	2	//	2	3165	40	//	14	//	3	8	00
Aug.	5	//	3	2256	10	Sept.	30	//	4	1180	00
Sept.	30	//	4	4835	80	//	//	//	4	840	00
						//	//	//	5	6103	75
				16554	55					16554	55
Sept.	30	J.	5	6103	75						

Dr. | Profit & Loss | **Cr.**

1851						1851					
Sept.	30	J.	4	944	00	Sept.	30	J.	4	2529	79
//	//	//	5	1585	79						
				2529	79					2529	79

Dr. | Balance | **Cr.**

1851						1851					
Sept.	30	J.	5	11585	79	Sept.	30	J.	5	11585	79
//	//	J.	5	11585	79	//	//	J.	5	11585	79

Dr. | Hill & Wright | **Cr.**

1851						1851					
Aug.	6	J.	3	3420	00	Apr.	1	J.	1	4600	00
Sept.	30	//	4	1180	00						
				4600	00					4600	00

1851						1851						
Apr.	1	J.	1	3500	00	July	2	J.	2	3165	40
Aug.	27	''	3	1912	45	Sept.	30	''	4	2247	05
				5412	45					5412	45

Dr. S. C. Woodward & Co. Cr.

1851						1851						
Apr.	15	J.	1	1250	00	June	24	J.	2	1250	00
Aug.	25	''	3	2280	00	Sept.	30	''	5	2280	00
				3530	00					3530	00
1851											
Sept.	30	J.	5	2280	00						

Dr.　　Clark & Smith　　Cr.

1851						1851						
May	2	J.	1	980	50	Aug.	5	J.	3	2256	10
July	21	''	2	1275	60	Sept.	30	''	5	1814	40
Sept.	10	''	4	1814	40						
				4070	50					4070	50
1851											
Sept.	30	J.	5	1814	40						

Dr.　　Jas. Armitage　*　Cr.

1851						1851						
May	15	J.	1	2106	00	Sept.	30	J.	4	2588	75
Aug.	5	''	3	482	75						
				2588	75					2588	75

Dr. *Trial Balance* **Cr.**

		Stock	10000	00
		Merchandise	1142	15
944	00	Expenses		
6103	75	Cash		
2280	00	S. C. Woodward & Co.		
1814	40	Clark & Smith		
11142	15		11142	15

Dr. *Balance* **Cr.**

1387	64	Merchandise		
6103	75	Cash		
2280	00	S. C. Woodward & Co.		
1814	40	Clark & Smith		
		Stock	11585	79
11585	79		11585	79

EXAMPLES FOR PRACTICE.

FOURTH FORM OF ACCOUNTS.

THE transactions in the Examples for Practice in Double Entry have been numbered consecutively to correspond with the Journal entries that will be required in their solution. These twenty-three transactions are of the same general character with the twenty-one entered in the preceding Journal. Seven additional entries will be required here, as there, in balancing the books and reopening the unsettled accounts, which, if numbered, will range from **24** to **30** inclusive, corresponding with the Journal entries in the example that has been worked out, from **22** to **28** inclusive.

The student should be able, before proceeding to enter the following transactions, having copied the first twenty-one entries in the preceding Journal, to lay the book aside, post them into the Ledger, make the seven additional Journal entries, post these, and thus balance the books and reopen the unclosed accounts as has been done.

The first half of the accompanying Blank Journal and Ledger for Double Entry might be devoted to the entry of the former example, and the remaining half to the solution of the transactions that follow.

Wednesday, January 1st, 1851.

Transaction 1. I commence business with the following effects: Merchandise in store, per inventory, $22,150.00; $390.50, in Cash; and two Notes, one against John Brown for $500.00, and the other against D. C. Cook for $715.80.

Tr. 2. I owe on account for Merchandise as follows: O. D. Brown $750.30, and N. E. Otis $1006.00.

State the substance of the paragraph relating to the solution of the Examples for Practice in Double Entry. What should the student be able to do?

Monday, January 20th, 1851.

Tr. 3. I have this day sold to J. C. Sterling Mdse. on acct. as per Sales Book B, page 20th, amounting to $2250.40.

Monday, February 10th, 1851.

Tr. 4. I have this day sold to John Cooper Mdse. on acct. as per Sales Book B, page 56th, amounting to $1756.85.

Monday, February 24th, 1851.

Tr. 5. I have this day paid in Cash $650.00 Store Rent for six months from the first of January last, and $50.00 for one month's Clerk Hire.

Saturday, March 1st, 1851.

Tr. 6. I have this day sold to J. D. Morton Mdse. on acct. as per Sales Book B, page 75th, amounting to $4561.80.

Monday, March 10th, 1851.

Tr. 7. I have this day sold to Cook and Hall Mdse. on acct. as per Sales Book B, page 102d, amounting to $5645.00.

Monday, March 24th, 1851.

Tr. 8. I have this day sold to Wm. White Mdse. on acct. as per Sales Book B, page 140th, amounting to $1640.50.

Monday, March 31st, 1851.

Tr. 9. D. C. Cook has this day paid the Note I held against him for $715.80.

Thursday, April 3d, 1851.

Tr. 10. I have this day paid $820.40 in Cash for Merchandise bought, as per Invoice No. 3.

Thursday, April 17th, 1851.

Tr. 11. My Expenses to N. York to buy goods have been $25.50 ; Freight on Merchandise bought is $48.10 ; and I have bought one set of Account Books for $14.00; for each and all of which I have paid the Cash.

Saturday, April 28th, 1851.

Tr. 12. John Cooper has this day paid me $1256.50 in Cash, on account of Merchandise bought February 10th.

Thursday, May 1st, 1851.

Tr. 13. J. C. Sterling has this day paid me $1750.30 in Cash, on account of Merchandise bought January 20th.

Monday, May 19th, 1851.

Tr. 14. I have this day paid O. D. Brown $750.30 in Cash, in full of his Account.

Monday, June 2d, 1851.

Tr. 15. Cook and Hall have this day paid me $4500.00 in Cash, on account of Merchandise bought March 10th.

Monday, June 9th, 1851.

Tr. 16. I have this day sold to J. C. Sterling Mdse. on acct. as per Sales Book C, page 1st, amounting to $1244.80.

Monday, June 23d, 1851.

Tr. 17. John Brown has this day paid $351.81 on the Note I hold against him, and I have received an Annuity amounting to $83.00.

Thursday, June 26th, 1851.

Tr. 18. I have this day paid N. E. Otis $1006.00 in Cash, in full of his Account.

Saturday, June 28th, 1851.

Tr. 19. John Brown has this day paid me the balance due on his Note, the same being $148.19.

Monday, June 30th, 1851.

Tr. 20. J. D. Morton has this day paid me $4561.80 in Cash, in full of his Account for Merchandise bought March 1st.

Monday, July 14th, 1851.

Tr. 21. I have this day sold to Wm. White Mdse. on acct. as per Sales Book C, page 23d, amounting to $275.87.

Monday, July 21st, 1851.

Tr. 22. Cook and Hall have this day paid me $1145.00 in full of their Account for Merchandise bought March 10th.

Wednesday, July 30th, 1851.

Tr. 23. I have this day paid Cash for Store Expenses as follows: For Clerk Hire six months, $300.00 ; for Fuel and Lights, $68.00.

On taking an Inventory of goods remaining unsold, I find I have on hand Merchandise to the value of $9995.18.

1st. What has been the net gain in trade for the period of seven months, as derived from the preceding transactions?

2d. On balancing all the accounts of the Ledger and reopening those that are unsettled, what are the Dr. and Cr. amounts as exhibited in the Balance? *Ans.* 1st. Net gain, $3327.40.

Ans. 2d.

Balance.

Dr.				Cr.	
9995	18	Merchandise,			
11170	60	Cash,			
1744	90	J. C. Sterling,			
500	35	John Cooper,			
1916	37	Wm. White,			
		Stock, - - -		25327	40
25327	40			25327	40

MAYHEW ON POPULAR EDUCATION.

This work was prepared in accordance with a resolution of the Legislature of Michigan. The following are but a specimen of scores of similar notices of it that might be presented, did space permit:

We have read most of the works of this character which have been published in this country, and while we feel that comparisons are commonly odious, we are free to acknowledge that we have not before read a book which so ably discusses almost every topic connected with Popular Education. * * Take it as a whole, we have never before seen its equal.—*New York Journal of Education.*

We commend the work, not merely as a useful manual for teachers and school committees, but as one TO BE READ BY THE PEOPLE—every man, woman, and child of whom is interested in the subject of which it treats.—*Methodist Quarterly Review.*

A valuable treatise on the subject to which it is devoted, discussing it, in its various details, with great comprehensiveness of view, with a rich copiousness of illustration, and with excellent common sense.—*New York Tribune.*

No greater service could be done to the commonwealth than to put a copy of this work into every one of its families.—*Michigan Farmer.*

It is a rich concentration of the best principles on the noblest of subjects; and the man who can make its truths familiar to the minds and operative upon the actions of our people, is their highest benefactor.—*Rev. D. D. Whedon, D.D.*

Every Parent should have a copy of it. Each Teacher of our youth should be familiar with its whole contents. I do not know of a book upon that subject, in the world, which is so proper to be used as a textbook in all our higher seminaries.—*Rev. E. Cheever.*

It is a work for circulation; and the friends of free education could hardly do a better thing than to set the volume freely at work in the community at large.—*New York Evangelist.*

For worth and ability this work even surpasses our anticipations. It is peculiarly *the work* to be *studied* by the whole people.—*Eclectic Journal of Education.*

It may properly be regarded as a FAMILY BOOK, furnishing an amount of varied instruction and entertainment to the intelligent households of our countrymen, for which they will be sincerely grateful.—*Christian Quarterly Review.*

MAYHEW'S PRACTICAL BOOK-KEEPING,

BY SINGLE AND DOUBLE ENTRY.

The title of this volume—*Practical Book-keeping*—is indicative of its leading characteristics. The specimens of accounts presented in it are in script, that closely resembles writing, and they hence afford excellent models for imitation. The book contains four forms of accounts, immediately following each of which is a large number of examples for practice. In their solution the pupil has occasion practically to apply the knowledge he has already acquired of both arithmetic and penmanship, while at the same time he learns Book-keeping as he will have occasion to practice it in after life. That this treatise ought to be as extensively studied in all our schools as arithmetic, grammar, and geography now are, is a commonly received opinion among practical educators to whom it has become known.

" I have examined with considerable attention Mayhew's Practical Book-keeping, designed to be used in the instruction of common schools. It is better adapted, in my judgment, to the ordinary business of the great majority of the people of our country than any treatise that has hitherto been used. It is calculated to bring into use the knowledge the pupil has acquired of arithmetic and penmanship. It furnishes a systematic method for the transaction of the common business of life, and cannot fail, I think, to be received with favor by teachers and others throughout the country. I feel greatly disposed to favor its use."   JOSEPH McKEEN,
Sup't Com. Schools for the City and County of New York.

" I have given a thorough examination to the plan of Mayhew's Practical Book-keeping, and to his method of carrying out that plan, and both meet my entire and unqualified approbation. Admirably adapted to meet the wants of scholars of both sexes, it is the only work that suits my views as calculated for young ladies. It makes practical the knowledge previously gained in arithmetic, teaches the pupil business composition, and lays open in a singularly clear and concise manner the whole theory of account-keeping and business transactions. Its study will make girls better *helpmeets*, as wife, sister, or daughter, to the farmer, mechanic, or professional man, than without the knowledge it imparts they could possibly be. It is adopted as the text-book on the subject in this institution."
JOHN B. NEWMAN,
President of Harrodsburg Female College, Harrodsburg, Ky.

785581

Printed in Great Britain by
Amazon.co.uk, Ltd.,
Marston Gate.